KU-334-913

International Meat Cookery

Colour Library of Step by Step Cookery

International Meat Cookery

Translated and adapted by Marie-Christine Comte
With an introduction by Gill Edden

ORBIS BOOKS·LONDON

Contents

Photographs by C. Mariorossi
Recipes adapted from l'Unil-It, SpA
ISBN 0 85613 172 5

Foreword

Meat is our highest quality protein food. All varieties of meat, whether farmed or wild, four footed or winged, are important sources of nutrition – and of gastronomic pleasure. The killing, dressing, buying and cooking of meats of all kinds are amongst the most skilful arts of all concerned with food, for the flavour and texture of meat is always different and is very largely dependent on the way the beast or bird is treated before it reaches the table.

Fortunately, few housewives now need to know how to kill and dress meat, how to butcher it or how long to hang it – this is knowledge special to the butchery trade. It is, however, important to be able to buy well from your butcher and for that purpose it is best to go regularly to one tradesman who will get to know you and who will be pleased to advise you. Supermarket meat is often cheaper than that offered in the butcher's shop, but you will not have the advantage of specialist knowledge from the assistant serving you.

Buying well does not necessarily mean buying expensively; cheap cuts can taste excellent if properly cooked. The secret is in knowing exactly what you have bought and the best way to cook it. We hope that with the help of this volume you will be able to serve your family and guests with some of the finest meals they have tasted.

The Colour Library of Step by Step Cookery will cover the whole range of good cooking. Each book is complete in itself and together they take you from the start of a meal to the end. In them we describe the preparation of dishes with the greatest care and include plenty of detailed information about the foods used, their nutritional values and how to make the best of them. You will find few short cuts – our recipes are based mainly on traditional French and Italian cooking – but anyone who takes the trouble to follow our methods will have earned a right to the prestige that goes with 'keeping a good table'.

Each volume in the series contains a glossary of the special cooking terms used. In the course of the series we shall cover everything you need to know about meal planning, garnishes, herbs and spices and the preparation of all kinds of foods. We haven't neglected drinks and preserving is also included. The basis of good cooking is an international tradition. It is a skill that is fundamental to home-making and to successful entertaining alike.

Glossary

Al dente
Italian expression used to mean just tender but not soft ('to the tooth'). To test, press the food (usually pasta or rice) with the thumbnail; it should cut cleanly.

Baste, to
To spoon hot liquid over food as it cooks, to keep it moist and flavoursome.

Beef marrow
The bones, particularly the shank bones of a bullock or calf, are filled with a softish substance called marrow. When the bones are cooked for stock it is the marrow which helps to make a good jelly. The marrow can also be scooped out of the bone and used as a nourishing ingredient in dishes.

Beurre manié
Butter kneaded with flour for use as a liaison. The butter and flour are kneaded together on a plate and added in small pieces to the hot liquid. As each piece is stirred in it cooks and thickens the liquid. This method of thickening has the advantage that it can be done a little at a time, making it easy to avoid over-thickening.

Bouquet garni
Bundle of herbs, traditionally tied together with string round their stalks, but now more usually wrapped in muslin. The herbs are removed from the dish before it is served. Bouquets garnis of dried herbs are often sold in sachets.

Brochette, en
Small pieces of meat, fish or poultry and vegetables grilled together on a skewer (as for kebab).

Condiments
Spices or seasonings served at the table to add flavour to a dish, e.g. salt, pepper, mustard and bottled sauces.

Consommé
Clear soup of concentrated, clarified beef stock. May be served hot with various garnishes or cold; when cold a consommé should turn to jelly.

Croquette
A savoury mixture bound together with a thick sauce, divided into balls or rounds, then generally dipped in beaten egg and breadcrumbs and deep fried.

Croûtons
Small pieces of bread or potato, toasted or fried and used as a garnish for a hot meat dish or soup.

Flame, to
To pour flaming spirit or fortified wine over food. The spirit must first be warmed so that it will ignite, then when it is alight it is poured over the food. This burns the alcohol out of the liquor but concentrates its flavour.

Grappa
Crude Italian spirit distilled from the skins, pips and stalks of grapes after they have been pressed for wine.

Gratiné, to
To brown the top of a dish. The food is generally sprinkled with breadcrumbs, butter and sometimes grated cheese, then placed in a hot oven or under a preheated grill to brown. A fireproof dish with handles at either end is known as a gratin dish.

Lard, to
To sew pieces of fat into a cut of meat with no fat of its own. A special larding needle is used for this purpose.

Marinate
To soak a food (usually meat, fish or poultry) in a flavoured liquid before cooking to make it more tender and add extra flavour. The liquid (marinade) is most commonly oil, vinegar or wine, salt, pepper and herbs or spices. The marinade is often cooked with the dish and served as a sauce.

Mortar
Small bowl, usually made of stone, wood or metal, used with a pestle for pounding and grinding small quantities of foods and spices.

Polenta
A maize meal used in bread, cakes and gnocchi. Semolina can usually be used as a substitute.

Reduce, to
To boil a liquid fast, thereby reducing the quantity and concentrating the flavour.

Sauté, to
To brown food quickly in butter or oil and butter. Sometimes cooking is finished in the sauce that is made with the food in the sauté pan.

Scald, to
To heat almost to boiling point.

Worcestershire sauce
Commercially made, bottled sauce based on soy sauce and well spiced. Used in flavouring meat dishes and pies.

Beef

How to cook cuts of beef

Top ribs	Braise
Rib roast	Roast or braise
Wing ribs	Roast
Sirloin	Roast or grill
Rump	Grill
Aitchbone	Roast or braise
Topside	Roast or braise
Buttock and silverside (fresh and salted)	Boil
Shin and cow heel	Stew
Thick flank	Stew, braise or boil
Thin flank	Stew, braise or boil
Brisket (fresh or salted)	Boil
Chuck steak	Stew or braise
Shin	Stew
Sticking piece	Stew
Clod	Stew
Neck	Stew

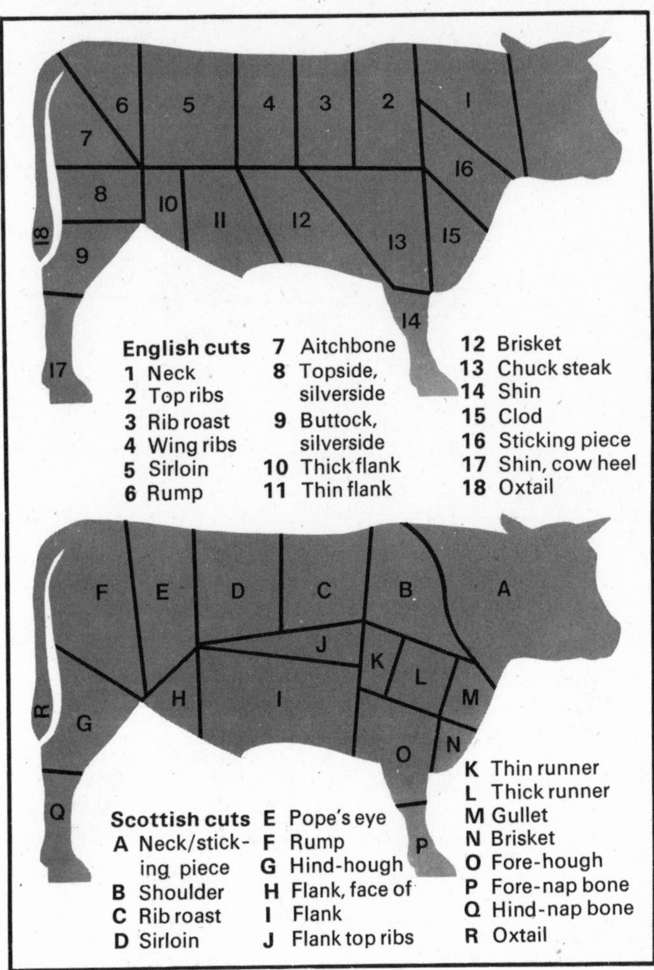

Roasting times for beef

On the bone	
375°F/gas 5	15 minutes per lb (500 g), plus 15 minutes (rare)
375°F/gas 5	20 minutes per lb (500 g), plus 20 minutes (medium)
375°F/gas 5	25 minutes per lb (500 g) (medium–well done)
Boned and rolled	
375°F/gas 5	20 minutes per lb (500 g), plus 20 minutes (rare)
375°F/gas 5	25 minutes per lb (500 g), plus 25 minutes (medium)
375°F/gas 5	30 minutes per lb (500 g) (medium–well done)

Roasting beef

Beef is very rich in protein, whether you choose one of the best roasting cuts or a more economical piece of shin for stewing.

It is traditional to serve roast beef slightly underdone, but this is only suitable for the best, most tender cuts, and of course not everybody likes it that way. Traditionally, roasting is carried out in the hot oven at 375°F/gas 5 in an open pan. The high temperature sears the meat quickly and seals in the juices, giving an excellent flavour. If you are not quite so confident of the quality of your roast, roast it more slowly at a less high oven temperature as this will ensure that the meat does not harden during cooking.

If you wish to cover the joint while roasting with a lid or with aluminium foil, in order to keep your oven cleaner, this will also help to keep the roast moist and succulent but it will not have quite the same traditional 'roast' flavour; if roasting covered, uncover the joint for the last 30 minutes of cooking time to brown the outside.

A brief guide to other ways of cooking meat is given on page 10.

A meat thermometer tells you even more accurately when your roast is cooked to your taste. The thermometer is inserted into the thickest part of the roast, taking care that it does not touch the bone. Using a meat thermometer you can even cook a frozen roast with confidence; simply start to cook the roast and insert the thermometer when it is sufficiently thawed. The temperature registered on the thermometer is the internal temperature of the meat so there can be no doubt that when the thermometer shows the required temperature, the meat is cooked. The following is a guide to using a thermometer to cook beef:

140°F – rare   160°F – medium
170°F – well done   180°F – very well done

Beef steaks

Steaks are cut from the sirloin, rump and adjacent cuts. They can be grilled or fried, the cooking time being the same for either method.
Rump steak has the best flavour but may not be quite as tender as other cuts unless it is really prime beef, well hung; it is normally cut about 1 inch thick.
Sirloin steak (also known as entrecôte) is cut from the top part of the sirloin. This is cut ¾–1 inch thick.
T-bone steak is a slice cut right across the sirloin, including the bone. This is normally cut 1½–2 inches thick and will weigh about 1½ lb (750 g). One side of the T-bone the meat is very tender, the other not quite so good.
Minute steak is a thin slice of sirloin steak, cut about ½ inch thick. It should be cooked very quickly (hence the name) so that it does not dry out.
Fillet steak is usually the most expensive to buy and the most tender to eat. The fillet is a small portion which lies under the sirloin and is cut in slices 1–1½ inches thick. There is no fat on fillet steak.

Cooking times for steaks

Rump	6–7 minutes	Rare
	8–10 minutes	Medium
	15 minutes	Well done
Sirloin	5 minutes	Rare
	6–7 minutes	Medium
	9–10 minutes	Well done
T-bone	7–8 minutes	Rare
	8–10 minutes	Medium
	13–15 minutes	Well done
Minute	1–1½ minutes	Rare
	2–3 minutes	Medium
	It dries out if cooked too well	
Fillet and Tournedos	6 minutes	Rare
	7–8 minutes	Medium
	9–10 minutes	Well done
Chateaubriand	16–20 minutes	Rare/medium
Porterhouse	7–8 minutes	Rare
	8–10 minutes	Medium
	13–15 minutes	Well done

Tournedos is a small round cut from the centre of the fillet, the same thickness as a fillet steak, but with the edges trimmed off.
Chateaubriand is a piece 3–4 inches thick cut from the heart of the fillet. It is cooked in the piece and sliced downwards for serving.
Porterhouse steak is cut from the wing rib, without bone. It is cut 1½–2 inches thick.

Veal

Cooking and serving veal

Veal is butchered into the same cuts as lamb, though the leg is known as fillet.

Because a veal animal is so young there is virtually no fat in the meat so it takes careful cooking to prevent drying and shrivelling up. Roast on the bone at 375°F/gas 5 for 25 minutes per lb (500 g), plus 25 minutes; off the bone, rolled, roast at the same temperature for 30 minutes per lb (500 g), plus 30 minutes. 175°F on the thermometer indicates the joint is cooked.

Apart from roasting, the most popular ways of serving veal are in pies, often accompanied by ham for extra flavour, as escalopes and many variations on the traditional fried escalope, coated in egg and crumbs, known as a Wiener Schnitzel.

How to cook cuts of veal

Loin	Roast, braise or grill/fry as chops
Best end of neck	Roast, braise or stew; sauté or fry as cutlets
Scrag end of neck	Make into pies
Shoulder	Roast or stew
Breast	Roast
Fillet	Roast or fry as escalopes

Lamb

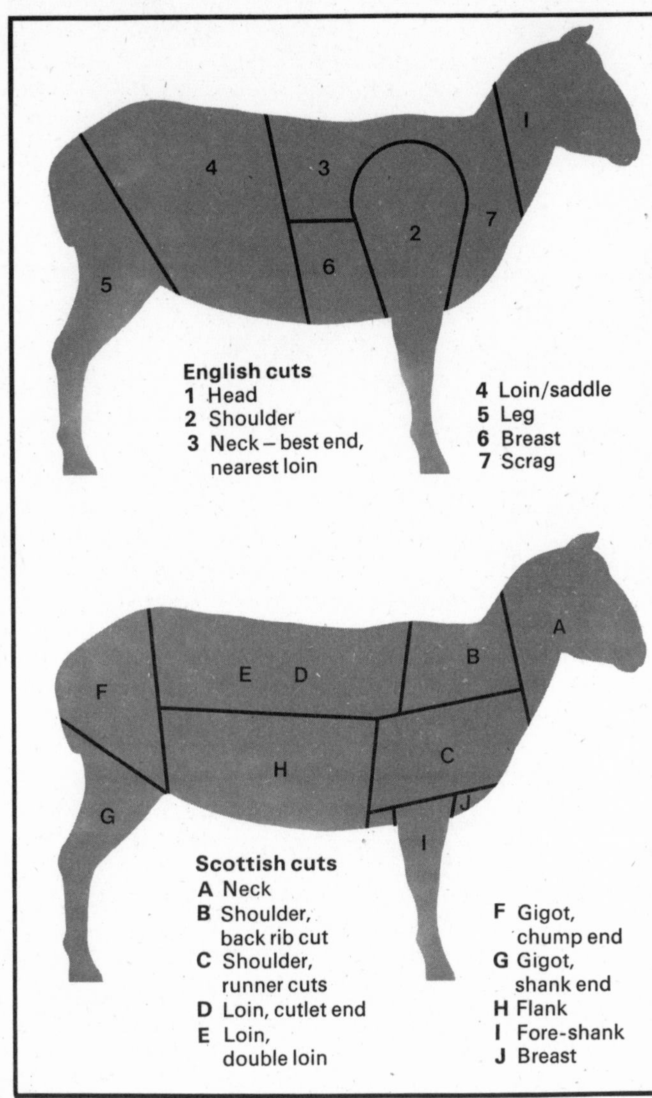

How to cook cuts of lamb

Loin or saddle	Roast, braise or grill as chops
Best end of neck	Roast or grill as cutlets
Scrag end of neck	Stew
Head	Broth
Shoulder	Roast or braise
Breast	Braise or stew
Leg	Roast or braise

Roasting times for lamb (to give a well done roast)

On the bone	
425°F/gas 7	20 minutes per lb (500 g) plus 20 minutes
350°F/gas 4	27 minutes per lb (500 g) plus 27 minutes
Boned and rolled	
425°F/gas 7	25 minutes per lb (500 g) plus 25 minutes
350°F/gas 4	35 minutes per lb (500 g) plus 25 minutes

Grilling times for lamb

Cutlets and noisettes	7–8 minutes
Loin chops	10–12 minutes (more if very large)

Cooking and serving lamb

The leg and loin are the meatiest roasts on a lamb (a saddle is the loin from both sides of the animal, still joined) and both roast well. A very small joint, but with choice, tender meat, is the best end of neck; this can also be cut into small cutlets for entrées. It is the best end of neck that is used for a traditional crown roast of lamb and for a *carré* (see p.44). The shoulder is slightly fattier than the leg or loin, but the meat is sweet, moist and tasty and many people prefer this joint. Scrag end of neck and breast of lamb both have a lot of bone and fat. Scrag makes excellent stews, but the fat should be skimmed off the cooked dish before it is served; the dish will be more pleasant if the bones are removed. Breast of lamb is usually boned and rolled before cooking, otherwise it is an unwieldy joint; occasionally it is stuffed and roasted.

Lamb is usually served well done, though the French prefer it underdone. A reading of 175°F on a meat thermometer indicates a well cooked roast.

Cuts most used for grilling are the cutlets from the best end of the neck and chops from the loin. Chunks of boneless meat from the leg or shoulder are threaded on to barbecue skewers to make kebabs, and sometimes a slice is cut from the end of the leg for grilling. Best end cutlets may be boned and tied into a neat circle with string to make 'noisettes'.

Pork

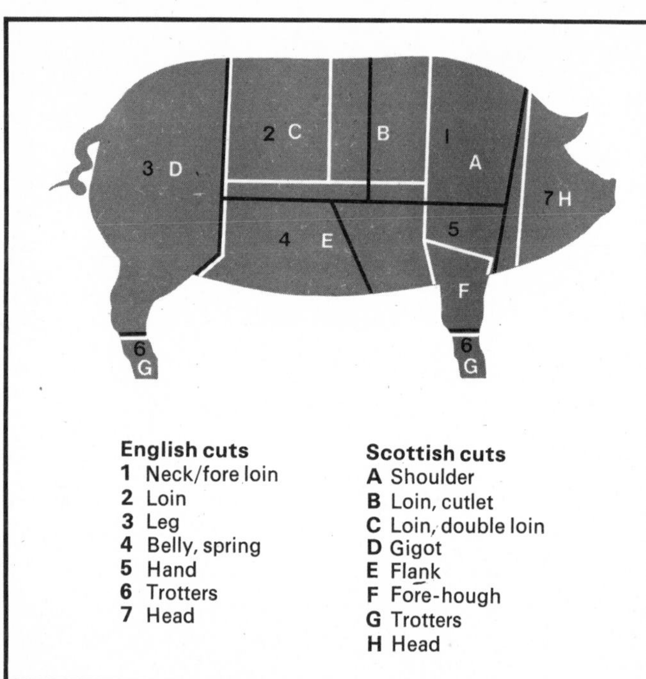

How to cook cuts of pork

Head	Boil (for brawn)
Trotters	Boil or braise
Hand and spring	Roast or boil
Belly (sold fresh or salted)	Boil
Leg	Roast
Loin	Roast or grill as chops
Neck or fore loin	Roast or braise

Cooking and serving pork

All pork should be well cooked. The leg and loin are the best cuts to roast, giving the best flavour; the hand is a succulent roast, but has less flavour. When the leg and loin are roasted, the skin is left on and served as 'crackling'. It is well scored, rubbed with oil and salt and when cooked becomes crisp and tasty; for serving, the crackling is removed from the joint first, the meat is carved and the crackling then divided up. Ask the butcher to chine the loin, to make carving easier.

Roast pork on the bone at 375°F/gas 5 for 25 minutes per lb (500 g), plus 25 minutes.

If the joint is boned and rolled, roast at 375°F/gas 5 for 30–35 minutes per lb (500 g), plus 35 minutes. A reading of 185°F on the meat thermometer indicates a moist but well cooked joint.

Pork is a very rich meat and to counteract this richness a sweet sauce such as apple or gooseberry is usually served with it. A boned and rolled joint is often stuffed with a savoury stuffing.

Loin chops are the best for grilling, and these should be well trimmed of surplus fat. Be careful to cook the chops for 12–15 minutes, until well cooked through.

To stew, braise or boil meat

To stew meat. For a brown stew first brown the meat, then take it out and add a little flour before nearly covering with hot stock; for white stew blanch the meat (not brown) and thicken liquid towards end of cooking. Liquid should simmer, not boil. Cook at 325°F/gas 3, or simmer on top of cooker for up to 2 hours, according to recipe.

For braising use a smaller quantity of liquid so that meat cooks more in the steam.

For boiling, do not brown meat but place in boiling water for 5 minutes, then simmer (20–25 minutes per lb (500 g) plus 20–25 minutes), skimming often.

Offal

Most offal, if cooked quickly, would be coarse in texture and flavour. But skilled preparation and long, slow cooking can produce dishes that are a true gastronomic delight and turn sweetbreads and kidneys, for instance, into delicacies of the table.

Offal should always be eaten very fresh. It should not be hung and should preferably be eaten on the day it is bought. It may be kept for 1–2 days in the refrigerator but should be well covered to prevent the smell contaminating other foods, and should be checked carefully before cooking; if in any doubt about the freshness, do not use it.

Most offal is nutritionally very good. Like all meats it is a source of protein; liver, particularly, is rich in iron and vitamins; kidney is also a good source of iron. Certain kinds of offal, chiefly the feet and stomach (tripe, pigs' trotters, cow heel, calves' feet), are very rich in gelatin. The feet are useful additions to stocks and casseroles to give a good, rich gravy. They may also be cooked as a meal in their own right but this is less common these days, as we seem to have lost the taste for gelatinous meats.

Preparation of offal

Liver
The livers of calves, oxen, pigs and sheep, as well as those of poultry and game, are all used. Calf's liver is the best, being very tender and delicate in flavour. It may be lightly grilled or fried. Lamb's liver is also good though a little stronger in flavour; this may also be grilled or fried and is good in casseroles. Pig's liver is generally used only for pâté. It has a strong flavour and a soft texture which many people do not like. Ox liver is usually the cheapest, being also the most coarse. It is too tough for frying or broiling, and should be casseroled or stewed; the flavor is quite strong.

Kidney
This is often used as a flavouring ingredient in a rich stew or pie. For this purpose ox kidney is ideal as the flavour is good and, the texture being a little coarse, it needs long, slow cooking to make it tender. Calf's kidney is more tender and more delicate in flavour than ox kidney, but is also used in stews; it is rarely tender enough to cook quickly. Lamb's kidney is very tender and grills well – this is a popular ingredient in a mixed grill. Pig's kidney will also grill, though it is not quite so tender.

Heart
The heart is usually stuffed and then either braised or roasted. Whichever animal the heart is from, slow cooking is to be recommended, though of course a lamb's heart will be more tender than an ox heart. Ox heart is sometimes sold sliced for including in stews and pies.

Tongue
Ox tongue is extremely popular served cold. The tongue is usually salted, then it is boiled gently with flavouring vegetables and pressed until cold. Calves' tongues may also be served like this. Lambs' tongues, however, are usually served hot, in a casserole. All tongues need a certain amount of extra preparation; they need soaking before cooking, trimming carefully and skinning.

Sweetbreads
A real luxury food, sweetbreads have a very delicate flavour and texture. Ox and calves' sweetbreads need slow, gentle cooking in a casserole to make them tender, but lambs' sweetbreads are tender enough to be fried or sautéed. Before cooking sweetbreads, soak them in cold water for 3–4 hours, then drain and put them into a pan. Cover with fresh cold water and a little lemon juice, bring to the boil and blanch them for 5 minutes. Drain them well, press to remove all surplus moisture and trim them to remove all the stringy tissue attached. They are then ready for cooking according to the recipe chosen.

Brains
Only calves' and lambs' brains are normally eaten, calves' being considered the best. Poached brains on toast is a very simple and popular dish, perhaps with a sauce, or brains may be stewed or casseroled.

Tripe
There are two types of tripe, known as 'blanket' and 'honeycomb', taken from the first and second stomachs of a beef animal respectively. There is no difference in the way they are cooked, or in the flavour, it is only the texture that is different. Tripe has to be cleaned very thoroughly and this is usually done by the butcher; he cleans it and partly cooks it before offering it for sale. Even so, tripe must be cooked for a long time to break down the strong cells and make the meat tender. Properly cooked and flavoured, tripe makes a delicious dish.

Spleen
Ox spleen is sometimes used in casseroles.

Poultry

Poultry is the general term used for all birds reared in the farmyard for eating purposes.

Chicken and turkey are white-fleshed birds with little natural fat; they are suitable for grilling, roasting, frying or casseroling. Duck and goose are darker-fleshed and have a thick covering of fat under the skin. These are best roasted or pot roasted so as to keep the skin crisp; as much of the fat as possible is drained off during cooking and a sharp sauce served with the meat to counteract the richness.

When selecting a bird for roasting, watch the following points. The flesh should be firm, the legs soft and free from scales. The wings and the tip of the breast bone should be pliable (in birds less than a year old the tip of the breast bone will still be cartilage; if it has hardened into bone this denotes an older bird). There should be a small amount of fat on the back, and a good fleshy breast; too much fat should be avoided. The skin and shanks may be white or yellow according to breed but either way they should be a good even colour, with no signs of bruising. Some birds even have blue shanks but these are rarely offered for sale by a poulterer because they look unattractive; if you are offered one privately, however, the flesh will taste just as good.

Don't forget when you buy a chicken ready dressed by the poulterer to ask for the giblets and preferably also the neck and feet. The liver is a delicacy that can be prepared in many tasty ways, while the kidney, heart, gizzard, neck, feet and wing tips will make an excellent stock for soup and other dishes. If the neck and feet are not available, the rest of the giblets will make tasty stock but it will not have the jellying quality supplied by the feet.

Trussing

Most birds need to be trussed if cooked whole, to keep them in good shape. The simplest way to truss is using skewers and string.

For a chicken, a not very large skewer is inserted right through the body just below the thigh bone; for a larger bird 2 skewers will be necessary, one on either side. Next turn the bird over on to its breast; pass the string under the protruding ends of the skewers, catching in the wing tips, and cross it over the back. Turn the bird over and tie the ends of the string round the tail, holding the drumsticks in place.

A more complicated way to truss, but much firmer and really the better method, is using a trussing needle threaded with fine string. The needle is inserted close to the second joint of one wing; it is pushed right through the body and brought out in the corresponding place on the other side. It is then re-inserted, this time into the first joint of the wing, through the flesh at the back of the body and catching in the wing tips and neck skin, to come out in the first joint of the wing on the other side. The ends of the string are tied in a bow. Then the needle is re-threaded to secure the legs; it is inserted through the gristle beside the parson's nose and the legs and tail are tied firmly together.

Always remember to remove the trussing string before serving up the bird.

Types of Chicken

Poussin
This term means a very young chicken weighing not more than 2 lb (1 kg). A really small one will serve only 1 person, a larger one will serve 2. Poussins should be roasted, grilled or pot roasted.

Spring chicken
Also known as broilers, these birds weigh about 3 lb ($1\frac{1}{2}$ kg), and will serve 3–4 people. These are suitable for roasting or pot roasting, sautés and casseroles. Most frozen chickens are broilers.

Roaster
These are chickens weighing from about 3 lb ($1\frac{1}{2}$ kg)–$5\frac{1}{2}$ lb ($2\frac{1}{2}$ kg) weight and therefore make excellent, tender meat for roasting while serving more people than a spring chicken. As well as roasting they may of course be boiled or pot roasted.

Boiler
Chickens of over 1 year old are more suitable for boiling, as the flesh will be less tender and more fatty. A boiler may weigh anything from 4 lb (2 kg).

Capon
As adult male birds do not normally make good eating, so young cocks not required for breeding are castrated and fattened specially for the table. The result is a much larger bird than a chicken – up to 8 lb (4 kg) – and excellent, tender meat for roasting.

Turkey

A good, fully grown turkey may weigh up to 40 lb ($18\frac{1}{2}$ kg), but many small breeds are produced which may be put on sale at 10 lb (4 kg). As with chicken, the hen bird is the more tender, with less bone in proportion to flesh; they are best eaten at 7–9 months old. When choosing a turkey, look for good, white flesh, a broad, plump breast and a short neck.

Duck

The term duck may refer to all sorts of swimming bird (see also Game), but when considering it as a form of poultry we are generally referring to the mallard, bred specially for the table; these birds will usually have done little swimming, and that will all have been in fresh water, and they will have been provided with food. The food a bird eats has a considerable effect on the flavour of its flesh and there is therefore a world of difference between the domesticated duck and the wild duck which has to grab what food it can.

When buying duck, look for a good, broad, meaty breast. There is a large proportion of bone to flesh on any duck and a 4-lb (2-kg) bird (dressed weight) will serve only 4 people.

There is plenty of fat on a duck so you will not need to add any to the roasting tin, as you would for chicken. The bird should be turned every 20 minutes or so during cooking, to ensure that the whole of the skin becomes crisp. Many people like to prick the skin during cooking so that the fat escapes and can be poured away; this takes some of the richness from the meat.

Goose

Geese very quickly run to fat and become tough. It is therefore very important when choosing one for the table to pick a young bird. This should still have a little down on its legs, and the legs should be soft and pliable.

The liver of the goose is of course much prized as the chief ingredient in pâté de foie gras. Although true foie gras is obtained only from force-fed geese an ordinary goose liver will still make good pâté.

A goose is cooked in much the same way as duck and is usually stuffed with a savoury stuffing of sage and onion, to counteract the richness of the flesh.

The size of a goose depends on the breed: 10 lb (4 kg) is usual, but the larger breeds may reach up to twice that weight after fattening.

Game

The term game covers all wild birds and animals hunted and killed for food. Here most game is protected from hunters by law during the breeding season and when the animals are young and very small; the exceptions to this are rabbit, hare and pigeon on which there is no restriction. Also sold with game, and cooked in similar ways, are the rabbits bred for the table and squabs, which are specially reared pigeons. Many birds eaten as game in other parts of the world are completely protected here.

Game falls into three groups. First are the small birds; these are not drawn before eating, but roasted or grilled, entrails and all, when very fresh – 'when the gun is smoking' is the traditional expression. Since they are only generally obtainable frozen or canned, this rule no longer carries any practical meaning.

The larger birds are perhaps the most important group of game, providing the most highly prized meats. This group includes many varieties of wild duck, pheasant, partridge and pigeon or squab. These are hung for several days to make the meat more tender and digestible. The joy of these birds, by contrast with poultry, is the variation in flavour which is produced by the food the bird has habitually eaten. For instance, a wild duck may be a sea bird and taste noticeably fishy, or it may be a fresh water bird and have taken amongst its food considerable amounts of plant and insect life. Although these are termed 'large' birds, they are not large by comparison with poultry.

The largest will usually serve only 4 people.

The last group of game consists of animals: hare, rabbit and deer (known in culinary terms as venison). Neither hare nor rabbit are protected. These meats have to be well hung to render them tender and tasty, and venison in particular is usually marinated as well before cooking.

Game seasons

The actual dates of the close seasons (when hunting is prohibited) are changed from time to time, to take into account changes in the habits of the animals and birds, how prolifically they are breeding and climatic trends.

Game sold at any other time of the year is invariably frozen. Wild rabbits are at their best in the winter, hare from late summer to spring.

Pheasant

Only the young birds are good for eating, and the huntsman detects the age of the bird by the shape of its wing tip – in young birds this is short and rounded and in older birds it becomes gradually more pointed and elongated. The hen is generally better than the cock, more tender and fatter.

Pheasant is hung by the neck undrawn and unplucked for anything from 3–10 days, depending on the weather and the condition of the bird after shooting and transportation. If the bird was carelessly shot, receiving a number of wounds, or if it was bruised at all in transportation, it should not be hung as long as one in perfect condition. If the bird is plucked and drawn before hanging, the flavour is nothing like as good.

A pheasant will serve 4 people.

Partridge

Young birds are best for roasting, and this means birds in their first year. These are again distinguished by their wings, the first flight feathers being pointed instead of rounded as in the older birds. Partridges of 1–2 years old are still good to eat but should be braised or casseroled rather than roasted as they will not be so tender.

Partridges can be hung as for pheasants, though the usual time is only 3–6 days.

A partridge is a small bird, serving only 1–2 people.

Wild duck

There are innumerable varieties of wild duck, from the large mallard which serves 4–5 people, to the tiny teal which will just about serve 1 person. Widgeon is generally one of the most popular. It tends to keep away from the sea, preferring to feed on short, sweet grass, which gives it a more delicate flavour than many ducks.

Squab

A young pigeon or squab has very delicate flesh that is excellent roasted. An older one will make a good casserole or tasty pie. Unlike other game birds, pigeons are plucked before hanging. When they are drawn, the liver is left inside to give added flavour to the meat.

Hare and rabbit

Hare and rabbit are hung by the feet and drawn after hanging. The blood of the hare is collected for thickening the sauce with which it is served. When young, either of these animals may be roasted, but they are more commonly casseroled or 'jugged' as the flesh may be rather dry.

Index

Page references to photographs are printed in **heavy** type.

**Note: all quantities given are for 4 servings unless otherwise stated.
Approximate metric equivalents to all measures are given in brackets.**

2

3

eef

teak Tartare

gredients: *1¼ lb (600 g) raw fillet steak or* *np, minced · salt · freshly ground pepper ·* *rsley · 4 egg yolks · 4 tablespoons chopped* *on · 4 tablespoons capers · 4 teaspoons* *stard · oil · lemon · Worcestershire sauce*

vide the raw beef into 4 portions (step 1), ason with salt and pepper to taste. Chop the rsley (step 2) and sprinkle it over the meat. ke a hollow in each meat portion, and put raw egg yolk in each (step 3). Arrange on e edge of each plate 1 tablespoon chopped ion, 1 tablespoon capers and 1 teaspoon istard. Serve oil, lemon and Worcestershire uce separately.

amburgers

x in a bowl 1¼ lb (600 g) ground beef, 1 ely chopped onion, and salt and pepper to ste. Shape the mixture into a ball, and beat repeatedly against the bottom of the bowl. vide into 4, shape into patties, roll in flour d cook in a frying pan on high heat in 2 oz 0 g) butter or oil. Cook on both sides, lower e heat, and continue cooking more slowly itil done according to taste. Serve the hamrgers, covered with fried onion rings and read with tomato ketchup, in buns.

amburgers with arbecue Sauce

x in a bowl 1 lb (500 g) ground beef, 4 tableoons crushed cornflakes (optional), 2 tableoons grated onion, and salt and pepper to ste. Work the mixture as above and divide to 4 patties. Brown on both sides in 2 oz 0 g) butter or oil, and remove them from the n. Add to the cooking juices 1 onion and 1 lery stick, both sliced, 1 green pepper, deeded and cut into strips, 4 teaspoons ustard, a little stock and salt and pepper to ste. Cook for 10 minutes, then add the hamrgers and continue cooking on low heat for hour. Serve with the reduced sauce.

1

2

3

Steak alla Pizzaiola

Ingredients: *4 tender beef steaks · 2 oz (60 g) butter or 4 tablespoons oil · salt · pepper · 2 cloves of garlic, peeled · 10 oz (300 g) canned peeled tomatoes, roughly chopped · 1 generous pinch oregano*

To garnish: *parsley*

Brown the steaks on both sides in the butter or oil on high heat (step 1) and continue cooking according to taste. Remove them, place on a warm serving dish, and season with salt and pepper to taste. Cook the cloves of garlic in the juices remaining in the pan until golden, remove them, add the tomatoes (step 2), salt and pepper to taste, and oregano. Continue cooking for 8–10 minutes, put the steaks back into the pan (step 3), re-heat quickly, and serve, coated with some of the sauce, on the hot serving dish. Garnish with parsley and serve with remaining sauce.

Steak à la Bismarck

Brown on both sides, on high heat, 4 slices fillet steak (each about 6 oz/175 g) in 2 oz (60 g) butter or oil. Continue cooking according to taste. Season with salt and pepper to taste, arrange them on a hot serving dish, and keep warm. Place on each steak 1 egg, fried in 2 oz (60 g) butter. Add a few spoonfuls stock to the cooking juices of the meat, mix well, boil rapidly for a few seconds, then pour over the steaks. Serve immediately.

Steak Chasseur

Brown 4 tender steaks on both sides in 2 oz. (60 g) butter or oil on high heat, and continue cooking according to taste. Remove the steaks and put them on a warm dish. In the cooking juices remaining in the pan, cook 1 slice onion, chopped, and ½ lb (225 g) mushrooms, cleaned, trimmed and sliced, until golde
Stir in 1 glass dry white wine, a little stock ar
1 tablespoon tomato paste. Continue cooki
on low heat for 10–15 minutes, then retu
steaks to the pan to reheat, and add chopp
parsley.

Steak Lyonnaise

In 1 oz (30 g) butter cook until transparer
but not browned, 2 large onions very thin
sliced. Remove and reserve. Brown 4 stea
(about 6 oz/175 g each) on both sides in 2
(60 g) butter or oil on high heat. Contin
cooking according to taste. Season with salt a
pepper to taste halfway through the cookin
Remove the steaks from the pan and pla
on a warm serving dish. Add ½ glass d
white wine to the cooking juices, boil for
minutes, add the onions, and, as soon as th
are hot, pour over the steaks.

Fillet of Beef Stuffed with Mushrooms

Ingredients: *1 whole piece of fillet of beef, preferably the middle part (about 2 lb/1 kg) · ¼ pint (¼ l) dry white wine · 4 oz (225 g) butter or oil · 1 small glass brandy · 1 bay leaf · 1 pinch thyme (optional) · salt · 1 medium-sized onion, thinly sliced · 10 oz (300 g) fresh mushrooms, or 1½ tablespoons dried mushrooms, soaked in water, squeezed dry and sliced*

To garnish: *mushrooms · parsley*

Put the beef in a bowl, add the white wine, and leave to marinate overnight. Melt in a pan half the butter, add the brandy, bay leaf, thyme, and salt to taste. Add the onion and cook slowly until golden. Add the mushrooms and continue cooking. Meanwhile, drain the beef, reserving the marinade, and make an incision along the narrow side with a sharp knife (step 1). Stuff with the mushrooms (step 2), seal the two ends with 2 pieces of meat from the inside of the fillet, and tie the meat with string to keep the stuffing inside (step 3). Brown the fillet on all sides over high heat in the remaining butter or oil, baste it with some wine from the marinade, cover the pan, lower the heat, and continue cooking for about 40 minutes – or less, according to taste. Alternatively the fillet may be cooked in the oven. Baste with the cooking juices from time to time. Serve the steak sliced, with the cooking juices, and garnish with whole mushrooms sautéed in butter, and parsley.

Fillet of Beef with Olives

Put one 2-lb (1-kg) piece of fillet of beef in a baking pan with 2 oz (60 g) butter or oil. Place in a moderate oven (350°F/gas 4), and cook for 25–30 minutes, basting occasionally with dry white wine and stock. Brown in a separate pan 2 oz (60 g) butter mixed with 2 tablespoons flour, add the cooking juices of the meat, and continue cooking for 8–10 minutes, adding more wine and stock if necessary, until the sauce is smooth and creamy. Add about ½ lb (225 g) pitted green olives, pepper, a little salt, and, when the mixture is hot, some chopped parsley. When the fillet is cooked, slice it and arrange on a warm dish with the sauce.

Fillet of Beef with Parsley

Mix a few tablespoons oilve oil with chopped parsley and freshly ground pepper. Put into the mixture 1 whole piece of fillet of beef (2 lb/1 kg) and let stand for 24 hours, turning occasionally. Then put everything in a flameproof casserole, and cook on high heat for 20–25 minutes, or more according to taste. Halfway through the cooking time season with salt and pepper to taste, and add more chopped parsley. Add a few spoonfuls stock if the meat becomes too dry.

Slice the meat and serve immediately on a warm serving dish, covered with the cooking juices.

2

3

Fondue Bourguignonne

Cut 1 lb (500 g) fillet of beef into 1-inch cubes (step 1), removing any fat and gristle. Put in a small pan – the classic pans for this dish are usually made of copper – a generous measure of oil, 1 pinch of thyme or 1 bay leaf (optional) and bring slowly to the boil. Place the pan over a portable burner in the centre of the table so that it continues to boil.

Each guest spears a cube of meat with a long fork, dips it into the hot oil until cooked to taste, transfers it to his own plate and dips it into one of several sauces which accompany the dish. The sauces (see the following suggestions) should be prepared beforehand (steps 2 and 3).

Garlic Sauce
Crush in a mortar 1 head of garlic (about 1 oz/30 g). Mix with 1 raw egg yolk and 1 pinch salt in a bowl. Stirring constantly with a wooden spoon, pour in gradually 8 fl oz (200 ml) oil and the juice of 1 lemon, as for mayonnaise. If the sauce is too thick, dilute with a few drops hot water. If, on the contrary, the sauce does not stiffen, or curdles, beat a fresh egg yolk in a separate bowl and add the sauce to it gradually – again as for mayonnaise.

Andalusian Sauce
Roast 1 pepper in the oven or over a flame, peel and sauté it in a frying pan in a little oil with a pinch of salt, let cool, deseed it, and cut into thin strips. In a bowl, mix the strips with 1 cup mayonnaise, diluted with home-made tomato sauce, sieved, reduced and cooled.

Caper Sauce
Mix into 1 cup mayonnaise a handful of capers, and some gherkins, finely chopped.

Rémoulade Sauce
In a bowl, mix 1 cup mayonnaise with 4 gherkins and 1 tablespoon capers, finely chopped, $\frac{1}{4}$ teaspoon anchovy paste or $\frac{1}{2}$ teaspoon mustard, 1 teaspoon chervil, 1 teaspoon chopped parsley, 1 teaspoon chopped shallot, and 1 pinch cayenne pepper. Add salt if necessary.

Mustard Sauce
In a bowl mix 6 tablespoons mayonnaise with 2 tablespoons French mustard, and 2 chopped spring onions or 1 tablespoon chives.

Kishaili Sauce
In a bowl, mix 5 oz (150 g) fresh ricotta or cottage cheese with celery salt and pepper to taste, and enough oil and vinegar to obtain a smooth paste. Add 1 bunch radishes, washed, trimmed and sliced, and let stand 48 hours.

Aurore Sauce
In a bowl mix 1 cup mayonnaise with 1 t
spoon paprika, 2 tablespoons tomato ketch
1 tablespoon ground pine nuts, 1 tablespc
capers chopped with 1 slice onion and so
parsley, 1 tablespoon brandy, and salt.

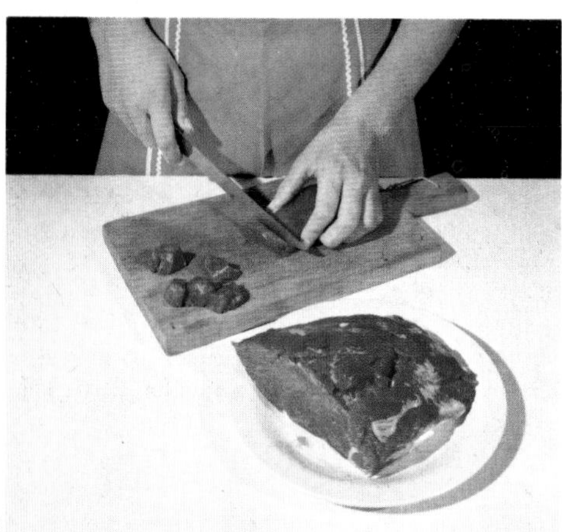

1

2

3

2

3

;randmother's Meat Loaf

gredients: *$1\frac{1}{2}$ lb (750 g) top rump of beef · slice mortadella (6 oz/175 g) · lb (340 g) frozen chopped spinach, thawed cording to package instructions (or fresh inach, cooked and worked through a sieve) · oz (60 g) butter or oil · 8 oz (225 g) :otta or cottage cheese · 1 egg yolk · tablespoons grated Parmesan cheese · salt · pper · nutmeg · 1 small glass Marsala or glass dry white wine · stock*

garnish: *carrots*

y the spinach over moderate heat with 1 (30 g) butter. When it has cooled, add the :otta or cottage cheese, the egg yolk, rmesan cheese, and salt, pepper and nut-eg to taste (step 1). Beat the meat well, it the mortadella slice on top, cover with the inach mixture (step 2), roll up, and sew it (step 3). Brown the loaf on all sides over high heat in 2 oz (60 g) butter or oil, add the Marsala or wine and let it reduce. Sprinkle the meat with salt, and add a little stock. Cover, lower the heat and cook slowly for about 2 hours, adding more stock if the meat becomes dry. Remove the loaf from the pan, let stand for 5–10 minutes, then slice, and arrange on a warm serving dish with the reduced cooking juices. Garnish with diced carrots. This dish is also very good when served cold – perhaps with aspic.

Meat Loaf with Frittata

Beat $1\frac{1}{2}$ lb (750 g) top rump of beef in the slice. Prepare a frittata (a flat, Italian-style omelet) in the following way: beat 2 eggs with 1 tablespoon chopped parsley, 2 tablespoons grated Parmesan cheese, 2 tablespoons milk, and salt and pepper to taste, and cook the mixture on both sides in 1 oz (30 g) butter or margarine, then let it cool. Place on the beef 1 or 2 slices cooked ham (each $\frac{1}{4}$ inch thick), the frittata, and a few slices Emmenthal cheese. Roll up the meat, tie with string, and brown on all sides over high heat in 2 oz (60 g) butter. Add 1 small glass brandy or grappa, and flame it, or add $\frac{1}{2}$ glass dry white wine and allow to reduce. Season with salt and pepper to taste, add a little stock, cover, lower the heat and cook slowly for about 2 hours, adding more stock if the meat becomes dry. Remove the loaf from the pan, let stand for 5–10 minutes, then slice it and arrange on a warm serving dish with the reduced cooking juices. Veal may equally well be used for this recipe as beef.

1

2

3

Mince Loaf

Ingredients: *$1\frac{1}{4}$ lb (600 g) mince · 4 oz (115 g) mortadella · 2 eggs · 1 handful white bread, soaked in milk and squeezed dry · $\frac{1}{2}$ lb (225 g) boiled potatoes (optional) · 2 tablespoons grated Parmesan cheese · parsley · salt · pepper · nutmeg · flour · 2 oz (60 g) butter or margarine · 2 tablespoons Marsala or dry white wine · hot stock · 3 hard-boiled eggs, shelled · 3 carrots, blanched*

To garnish: *petits pois*

Mix in a bowl the mince, chopped mortadella, eggs, bread, and the potatoes (if using) worked through a sieve, Parmesan cheese, chopped parsley, and salt, pepper and nutmeg to taste (step 1). Make a ball of the mixture and beat it repeatedly against the bottom of the bowl. Flatten the mixture on a board, place the hard-boiled eggs and carrots in the centre (step 2), and roll up, shaping it into a loaf. Roll it in flour (step 3), and brown on all sides on high heat in butter or margarine. Season with salt, sprinkle with Marsala or wine and when it has reduced, add the hot stock. Cover, lower the heat, and cook slowly for about 1 hour, adding more stock if the loaf becomes dry. Remove the loaf from the pan, let stand for 5–10 minutes, then slice it and arrange on a warm serving dish with some of the reduced cooking juices. Garnish with petits pois and serve cooking juices separately.

Meat Loaf Clementina

Mix in a bowl $1\frac{1}{4}$ lb (600 g) minced beef, 2 oz (60 g) chopped mortadella, 2 oz (60 g) grated Parmesan cheese, 1 egg, and salt, pepper and nutmeg to taste. Shape the mixture into a ball, and beat it repeatedly against the bottom of t bowl, then spread it about $\frac{1}{2}$ inch thick on piece of cloth. Put over the meat one $\frac{1}{2}$-in thick slice cooked ham, cut into strips, and hard-boiled eggs. Roll the meat, wrap it in t cloth and tie at both ends. Boil in a genero amount salted water for about 2 hours, toppi up with more hot water as it evaporates. Pr pare a sauce in the following way: cook in few spoonfuls hot oil in a pan 2 oz (60 mashed anchovy fillets until well blende without allowing them to brown. Add 1 tabl spoon chopped capers and some chopp parsley, and continue cooking slowly for a fe minutes. Remove the sauce from heat and a the juice of 1 lemon. Remove the loaf from th pan, let stand for 5–10 minutes, then slice and arrange on a warm serving dish, wi the sauce poured over. Serve with mash potato or green vegetables.

Roast Beef

ngredients: *2 lb (1 kg) joint of beef (sirloin, ump, fillet or rib) · 2 oz (60 g) melted butter · carrot and 1 onion, peeled and cut in quarters · alt · pepper*

'o garnish: *tiny whole potatoes, boiled*

'ie the meat with string (step 1), brush it with alf the butter (step 2) and place on a rack in a oasting pan with the carrot and onion. Put it n a very hot oven (450°F/gas 8) and cook for 5–30 minutes, turning it and basting ccasionally with the remaining butter (step 3). Do not puncture the meat during cooking: se 2 spoons to turn it over.) Sprinkle it with alt and pepper halfway through the cooking. 'o check whether the meat is done, prick it vith a fork: a drop of pink juice should escape. Vhen cooked, remove beef from the pan, untie, nd let stand. Pour off excess fat from the pan, iscard carrot and onion, then add a few ablespoons stock to the pan to detach the lazed cooking juices, and bring to the boil. lice the beef, arrange on a warm serving ish, and pour the gravy over, or, if preerred, serve it separately in a sauce boat. arnish the dish with tiny whole boiled otatoes if liked.

Roast beef can also be cooked in a pan on op of the stove: tie the meat with a sprig of osemary, and put it in the pan with 3–4 ablespoons oil. Brown on high heat on all ides, cover the pan, lower the heat, and ontinue cooking slowly for 15–20 minutes, prinkling the meat with salt and pepper alfway through the cooking. When cooked, emove the meat, let stand, then slice it, and erve as above.

Roast Beef in Salt

'ut at the bottom of a high and narrow pan lb (1 kg) rock salt. Place in the centre a 2-lb 1-kg) joint of beef and put another 4 lb (2 kg) ock salt around and above the meat, covering completely. Cover the pan and put in a hot ven (400°F/gas 6) for about $\frac{3}{4}$ hour. Overturn ne pan on a sheet of thick paper and crack ne salt crust with a hammer. Remove all the alt from the meat with a brush, and serve ne meat hot or cold. The salt can be used gain. Serves 6–8.

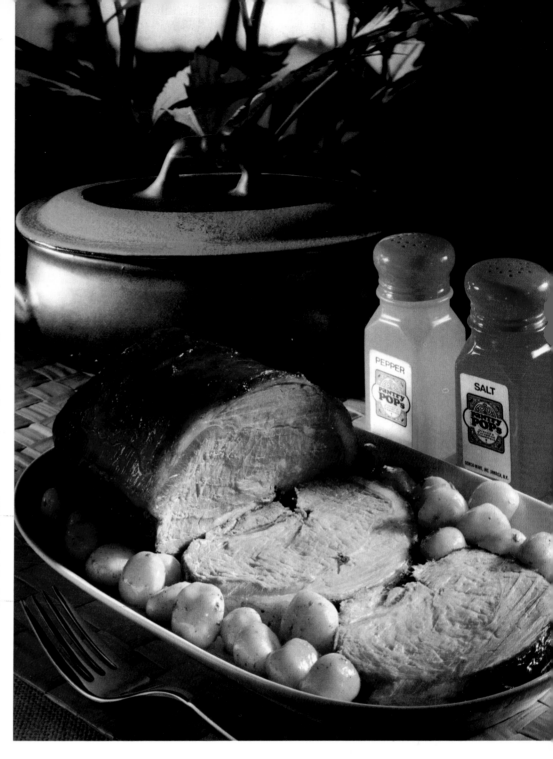

Roast Beef Croquettes

Chop 1 lb (500 g) rare roast beef and 7 oz (200 g) Italian prosciutto. Mix with chopped parsley and salt and pepper to taste. Form croquettes with the mixture, roll them in flour, brown them on all sides over high heat and cook them for a few minutes in butter.

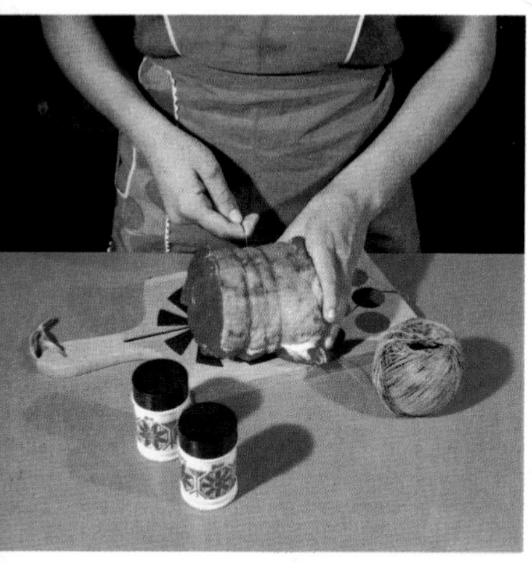

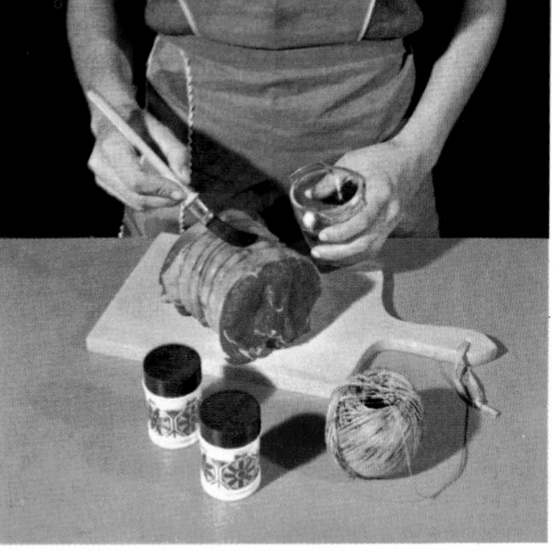

2

3

1

2

3

Beef Braised in Wine

Ingredients: *2 lb (1 kg) rump • 4 oz (115 g) salt pork • 2 oz (60 g) butter • 1 slice onion • flour • salt*

For the marinade: *1 pint ($\frac{1}{2}$ l) Burgundy-type wine • 1 stick celery • 1 onion and 1 carrot, both sliced • 1 clove of garlic, peeled and crushed • rosemary • 1 bay leaf • 3 peppercorns*

To garnish: *tiny whole potatoes, boiled • butter • parsley*

Lard the beef with half the salt pork (step 1), tie it with string, pour the prepared marinade over (step 2) and leave overnight. Chop the remaining salt pork, brown it in butter together with the onion. Drain the meat (reserving the marinade), dry it, roll in flour, add to the pan and brown on all sides over high heat (step 3). Add the reserved marinade, salt, cover, lower the heat and cook very slowly for about 3 hours. When cooked, remove the meat from the pan and let stand. Strain the sauce, boiling to reduce if too thin. Slice the meat and arrange on a warm serving dish with some of the sauce poured over. Serve the remaining sauce separately, and garnish the dish with tiny whole potatoes, tossed in butter and sprinkled with parsley.

Braised Beef

Lard 2 lb (1 kg) rump with strips of salt pork, chopped garlic (optional), and chopped parsley mixed with pepper and mixed herbs. Tie the meat with string, brown it on all sides over high heat in 1 oz (30 g) butter and 2 table spoons oil. Sprinkle with salt and pepper Add chopped celery, carrot and onion, 1 bou quet garni made of parsley, thyme and 1 ba leaf, and 1 small onion stuck with 1 clove. Pou in 1 cup good red wine, and 2 tablespoon brandy (optional). Cover the pan with wa paper or aluminium foil, lower heat, and coo very slowly for about 3 hours (or $1\frac{1}{4}$ hours in pressure cooker), turning the meat over wit 2 spoons occasionally. After 2 hours, strai the cooking juices, put them back into the par and thicken them with a little beurre man (equal parts of butter and flour, blende together). When the cooking is done, remov the meat from the sauce and let stand 5–1 minutes, slice, and arrange on a warm servin dish with the sauce poured over it. Serves

Tournedos Renata

ngredients: *4 slices fillet of beef, $1\frac{1}{2}$ inches hick · $\frac{1}{2}$ lb (225 g) butter · 2 lb (1 kg) ushrooms · 1 clove of garlic, peeled · salt · epper · 1 small glass brandy · 4 fl oz 100 ml) single cream · thyme · marjoram · mon · 1 tablespoon chopped parsley*

ut out 4 pats of butter – $\frac{1}{4}$ inch thick – with a mall round cutter (step 1), and keep them in he freezer or ice box. Trim the stems of the ushrooms, wash and dry, and slice them. rown the garlic in the butter then remove it; dd the mushrooms and sauté them quickly. dd salt and pepper to taste, pour in the randy, and flame it. Add half the cream, cover, ower the heat and cook slowly for about $\frac{1}{2}$ our. In the last few minutes add the rest of he cream, and prepare the tournedos. In a eparate pan, cook them quickly in 2 oz (60 g) browned butter, adding pepper, thyme, marjoram and salt to taste. Put the mushrooms in a warm oval serving dish, arrange the tournedos in the centre (step 2), and place over each 1 lemon slice and 1 pat of butter sprinkled with chopped parsley (step 3). Serve immediately.

Tournedos Rossini

Brown in 1 oz (30 g) butter 1 carrot and 1 small onion, both roughly chopped. Mix in 1 teaspoon flour, add $\frac{1}{4}$ pint (140 ml) stock, $\frac{1}{2}$ glass dry white wine, 1 bouquet garni made of parsley, thyme and bay leaf, and salt and pepper to taste. Cook very slowly for 25 minutes, then strain through a sieve. Fry 4 large bread croûtes in 2 oz (60 g) butter and keep warm on a serving dish. Cook in 2 oz (60 g) browned butter, on high heat, 4 tournedos for 2–3 minutes on each side. Season with salt and pepper to taste. Arrange them on the croûtes, and place on each 1 slice liver pâté and 1 slice truffle. (Where truffles are not easy to obtain, a flat mushroom may be substituted.) Dissolve the cooking juices in the pan with 1 small glass Madeira, and mix with the sauce. Pour some of the sauce over the tournedos, and serve immediately with the rest of the sauce separately.

2

3

1

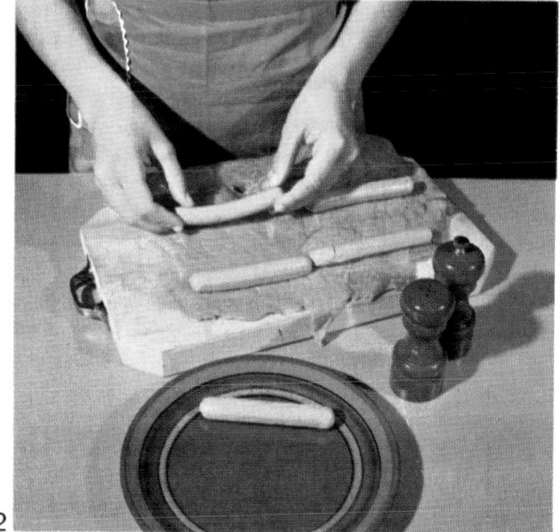
2

3

Veal

Rolled Veal with Frankfurters

Ingredients: *1½ lb (750 g) veal in the slice · 4 frankfurters · 2 oz (60 g) butter or oil · ½ glass dry white wine · salt · 4 fl oz (100 ml) hot stock*

Pound the meat slice (step 1), place the frankfurters over it lengthwise (step 2), roll and tie it with string (step 3). Brown on all sides over high heat in the butter or oil, add the white wine, and, when the wine has reduced, sprinkle the meat with salt, add the hot stock, cover, lower the heat, and cook slowly for 1½ hours. If there is too much juice, reduce it on high heat during the last minutes of cooking. Remove the roll from the pan and let stand 5–10 minutes. Slice it, arrange on a warm serving dish and pour the cooking juices over. The dish can also be served cold, in aspic, if desired. Beef can be used instead of veal.

Veal Loaf Cesira

Chop ½ lb (225 g) veal, mix it with 1 egg, 2 tablespoons grated Parmesan cheese, and salt and grated nutmeg to taste. Quarter 2 hard-boiled eggs and cut 3 oz (90 g) cooked ham and 3 oz (90 g) mortadella into strips. Pound 1½ lb (750 g) veal in the slice, spread over it a layer of the chopped meat mixture, then a layer of hard-boiled eggs, ham and mortadella strips, and continue until all the ingredients have been used. Roll the meat, tie with string, and brown on all sides over high heat in 2 oz (60 g) butter. Cover, lower the heat and cook for 1½ hours, adding stock occasionally. When cooked, lift out the loaf, add to the pan 2 tablespoons beurre manié (equal amounts of butter and flour worked together), the juice of 1 lemon and more stock if necessary. Cook for a few minutes, then return loaf to the pan and reheat. Transfer to a warm serving dish, slice, and serve with the juices poured over. Serves 4–6.

2

3

Stuffed Breast of Veal

ngredients: *2 lb (1 kg) breast of veal, boned · celery stalk · 1 onion, peeled and quartered · carrot, peeled and quartered · ½ bay leaf ·* *alt*

'or the stuffing: *1 slice onion · 2 oz (60 g) utter · 4 oz (115 g) lean veal · 4 oz (115 g) eal brains · 4 oz (115 g) sweetbreads · ¾ oz (50 g) marrow, scalded, skinned and cut nto pieces · 1 carrot, sliced · 6 oz (175 g) reen peas · 3 tablespoons grated Parmesan heese · 1 pinch marjoram (with a little garlic if esired) · 1 tablespoon pistachio nuts · salt · epper · grated nutmeg · 6 eggs*

'o garnish: *lettuce · tomatoes*

lave the butcher make a pocket in the breast f veal. Prepare the stuffing: sauté the onion 1 the butter (it can then be removed, according to taste), the veal, cut into thin slices, the brains, the sweetbreads, chopped, and the marrow. Add the carrot and cook slowly for 20–30 minutes. Add ⅓ of the green peas, cooked in boiling salted water, and divide the mixture into 2 parts. Work 1 part through a sieve, and chop the other part. Put both in a bowl, add the remaining green peas (step 1), the Parmesan cheese, marjoram, the pistachio nuts, scalded and peeled, and salt, pepper and nutmeg to taste. Beat the eggs, blend them into the mixture, and pour it – it will be fairly liquid – into the pocket cut in the breast of veal (step 2), taking care that it does not fill more than ⅔ of it. Sew it up with string (step 3) and wrap it in a wet piece of cloth. Tie well. Put in a pan, cover with cold water, add the celery, onion, carrot, bay leaf, and salt to taste, and bring slowly to the boil, pricking it occasionally with a trussing needle so that it does not burst as it swells. Continue cooking for about 2 hours, remove it from the stock, and put it on a plate with a weighted plate on top of it. Serve sliced, hot or cold, garnished with lettuce leaves and tomato slices. Serves 8. Any leftovers can be rolled in beaten egg and breadcrumbs, sautéed in butter and served with lemon quarters. Or they may be rolled in beaten egg and breadcrumbs, heated for a few minutes and served with green peas and home-made tomato sauce.

1

2

3

Roast Veal Sirloin

Ingredients: *2 lb (1 kg) veal sirloin · 2 oz (60 g) diced salt pork · chopped rosemary mixed with salt and pepper · 1 tablespoon oil · 2 oz (60 g) butter or margarine · salt · pepper · dry white wine (optional)*

To garnish: *green beans, sliced*

Make lengthwise incisions in the meat (step 1), roll the salt pork in the rosemary mixture (step 2), and insert in the meat (step 3). Tie the meat with string, brush it with the oil, and place it on a rack in a roasting pan, with the butter or margarine, in small pieces. Put the pan into a moderate oven (350°F/gas 4) and roast the meat for $1\frac{1}{2}$–$1\frac{3}{4}$ hours. When the meat is brown, sprinkle with salt and pepper, and dry white wine according to taste. Turn it over occasionally during the cooking, basting it with its own juices. When the meat is cooked, remove from pan, let stand for 5–10 minutes, then slice it and arrange on a warm serving dish.

Roast Veal in Piquant Sauce

Lard 2 lb (1 kg) veal sirloin with 2 cloves of garlic, peeled and sliced, and 4 anchovy fillets, desalted. (Shoulder of veal, boned, rolled and tied, may also be used for this recipe.) Put the meat in a bowl with 1 cup dry white wine and let stand for 24 hours, turning it over occasionally. Drain the meat, reserving the wine, brush with oil, place it on a rack in a roasting pan, and cook it for $1\frac{1}{2}$ hours in a moderate oven (350°F/gas 4). Baste frequently with the reserved wine. When the cooking is done, remove the meat, cover, and keep warm. Add to the pan 1 tablespoon flour mixed with a little cold water, stir with a wooden spoon to incorporate all the cooking juices, and continue cooking for a few minutes. Add $\frac{1}{4}$ pint (125 ml) single cream, 1 tablespoon washed and dried capers (whole if small, chopped if large), and heat the cream without boiling. Slice the meat and arrange on a warm serving dish. Serve the sauce separately. Serves 4–6.

Veal Pot Roast with Kidneys

Have the butcher bone 2 lb (1 kg) shoulder of veal. Halve 1 veal kidney lengthwise, let it stand in water and lemon juice for 1 hour, drain, and remove the membrane and skin. Put the 2 kidney pieces inside the roast, in place of the bone. Tie the meat with string, brush with oil, and put in a pan with 2 oz (60 g) butter or margarine in small pieces, and a sprig of rosemary. Brown it on all sides over high heat, pour over 1 small glass of brandy, and flame it. Cover, lower the heat, and cook on moderate heat for about 2 hours, adding a little stock occasionally if the meat becomes dry. Sprinkle with salt and pepper halfway through the cooking. When the cooking is completed, remove the meat from the pan, let stand for 5–10 minutes, then slice it and arrange on a warm serving dish with the reduced cooking juices poured over.

/lexican Paupiettes

ıgredients: *1¼ lb (600 g) veal cut into 8 ıall escalopes · 3 oz (90 g) pork loin · oz (90 g) prosciutto · ½ clove of garlic ptional) · 2 oz (60 g) white bread soaked in ilk and squeezed dry · 1 egg yolk · grated ımon peel · 1½ tablespoons grated Parmesan ıeese · salt · pepper · nutmeg · sage leaves · oz (90 g) butter or margarine · flour · stock*

ɔ serve: *mashed potato*

im and beat the veal escalopes (they should ː about 3 by 5 inches). Mince until very fine ıe pork loin, the prosciutto, the garlic (if ısing), and the bread. Mix in the egg yolk, ·ated lemon peel, Parmesan cheese, and salt, ·pper and nutmeg to taste. Blend the mixture ıoroughly, then spread over the meat slices ith a knife (step 1). Roll them up tightly, and ıck them 2 by 2 on toothpicks, with 1 sage ıaf between (step 2). Melt the butter or margarine in a pan, put in the paupiettes lightly coated with flour, and brown them on all sides over high heat. Add some stock (step 3), cover, lower the heat, and cook slowly for about ¾ hour, or until the paupiettes are cooked and the juice is reduced. Serve on a bed of mashed potato.

Italian Paupiettes

Trim 8 small veal escalopes (about 1¼ lb/600 g), and beat well. Chop 4 oz lean prosciutto, and mix it with 4 mashed and desalted anchovy fillets. Add 1 egg yolk, 3 tablespoons grated Parmesan cheese, and some grated white truffle (optional). Shape the mixture into 8 balls and put one in the centre of each meat slice. Roll the slices, tie with string, and brown them on all sides over high heat in 2 oz (60 g) butter or margarine. Cover, lower the heat and cook slowly for about 45 minutes. If you want to have a sauce add some stock during the cooking and let it reduce.

Florentine Paupiettes

Beat 8 small veal escalopes (about 1¼ lb/600 g). Trim the edges and chop the trimmings together with 4 oz (115 g) pork loin, a handful of spinach, celery, carrot and parsley. Cook the mixture in 2 oz (60 g) butter. Allow to cool, and mix with 1 egg, grated Parmesan cheese, and salt and grated nutmeg to taste. Spread the mixture over the meat slices, roll them, tie with string, and brown on all sides over high heat in 2 oz (60 g) butter or margarine with a little chopped onion. Sprinkle with salt, add 1 tablespoon tomato sauce diluted with a little water or stock, cover, lower the heat and cook slowly for about ¾ hour.

You could use beef instead of pork for the stuffing, in which case cook a little longer.

2

3

1

2

3

Ossobuco

Ingredients: *four 2-inch thick slices (about 2 lb/ 1 kg) of veal shank* (ossobuco) · *3 oz (90 g) butter or margarine* · *flour* · *$\frac{1}{2}$ glass dry white wine* · *1 celery stalk, 1 small carrot, $\frac{1}{2}$ onion, 2 desalted anchovy fillets, all chopped* · *salt* · *pepper* · *10 oz (300 g) canned peeled tomatoes, chopped* · *stock* · *garlic, parsley and the zest of $\frac{1}{2}$ lemon, all chopped*

To serve: *mashed potato or risotto*

Melt the butter or margarine in a pan, and immediately put in the floured veal slices (step 1). Brown them on all sides over high heat, add the dry white wine and let it reduce. Add the chopped celery, carrot, onion and anchovy fillets, and salt and pepper to taste. Cook until golden and add the tomatoes (step 2). Cover, lower the heat, and cook slowly for about $1\frac{1}{4}$ hours, adding stock occasionally to obtain a fairly thick juice. A few minutes before completing the cooking, add the chopped garlic, parsley and lemon zest to taste (step 3). Transfer to a warm serving dish and serve with mashed potatoes, or with a risotto.

Ossobuco with Mushrooms

Roll 4 slices of veal shank (about 2 lb/1 kg) in flour mixed with salt and pepper. Brown them on all sides over high heat in 2 oz (60 g) butter or margarine. Add $\frac{1}{2}$ glass dry white wine, let it reduce, then add chopped onion, carrot, garlic, parsley and grated lemon zest to taste, and 1 tablespoon dried mushrooms, soaked in lukewarm water and squeezed dry. Add tablespoons tomato sauce and some stoc Cover, lower the heat, and cook slowly fc about 1 hour.

Ossobuco with Green Peas

Brown 4 floured slices of veal shank (abou 2 lb/1 kg) on all sides over high heat, in 3 o (90 g) butter or margarine with 1 choppe onion. Sprinkle with salt. Add $\frac{1}{2}$ glass dr white wine, let it reduce, then add 6 oz (175 g canned peeled tomatoes, chopped, or som tomato sauce, a few ladles stock, and $1\frac{1}{4}$ l (600 g) fresh or frozen peas. Cover, lower th heat, and cook slowly for about 1 hour. Hal way through the cooking, add some hot wate if the juice is too thick.

Veal Escalopes with Ham

ıgredients: *4 veal escalopes (about 1 lb/500 g) · slices cooked ham · 4 slices Emmenthal heese · 4 small canned artichokes in oil · oz (60 g) butter or margarine · salt · cup dry white wine · 1 cup hot stock*

'o garnish: *artichoke hearts · peas · carrots*

'rim the veal slices, and beat well (step 1). over ½ of each slice with 1 slice of ham and 1 f cheese (step 2), and 1 artichoke cut into ıin slices. Fold the meat and seal the three pen sides with toothpicks (step 3). Brown the scalopes on all sides over high heat in butter r margarine. Sprinkle with salt. Add the ine, let it reduce, then add the stock. Cover, ›wer the heat, and cook slowly for 15–20 ıinutes. Serve garnished with artichoke earts and a macedoine of peas and carrots.

Veal Escalopes with Frankfurter and Cheese Stuffing

Trim 8 small veal escalopes and beat them. Put on 4 of them ½ slice Emmenthal cheese, ½ frankfurter (sliced lengthwise) and 1 teaspoon mustard. Cover them with the remaining escalopes, and press the edges together to seal them. Dip them in egg beaten with a little salt and breadcrumbs. Let them stand for ½ hour, then brown on all sides over high heat in 3 oz (90 g) butter or margarine. Cover, lower the heat, and cook slowly until golden.

Veal Escalopes with Prosciutto Stuffing

Trim 8 small escalopes of veal (about 1 lb/500 g) and beat well. Put on each escalope 1 slice prosciutto and 1 sage leaf, sprinkle with lemon juice, season with salt and pepper, then fold it. Close with toothpicks. Cook until golden and cooked through on high heat in oil mixed with butter, or in a moderate oven, as above. Thin slices of fillet of beef can also be used for this recipe.

Cutlets with Cheese Stuffing

Make an incision along the side of 4 veal or pork cutlets, without cutting all the way through. Insert 1 slice Emmenthal cheese and 2 sage leaves. Press the edges of the incision together to seal. Brown the cutlets on both sides over high heat in 1 oz (30 g) butter or margarine with 2 sage leaves. Season with salt and pepper to taste, cover, lower the heat, and cook for 20–25 minutes.

2

3

Saltimbocca alla Romana

Ingredients: *8 small veal escalopes (about $1\frac{1}{4}$ lb/600 g) · salt · pepper · 8 slices prosciutto (both the lean and the fat) · flour · 2 oz (60 g) butter or margarine · 8 sage leaves · dry white wine*

To garnish: *tiny whole potatoes, boiled*

Trim the veal escalopes, and beat, makin them all roughly the same size. Season wit salt and pepper (step 1), and put on each sage leaf. Cover with 1 slice prosciutto (step 2 and fasten with a toothpick (step 3). Dip then lightly in flour. Melt half the butter or margar ine in a pan, add the meat slices side by side increase the heat, and brown on both sides Continue cooking for a few minutes, unti golden and cooked through. Put on a warn serving dish and remove the toothpicks. Ad the wine to the cooking juices, and let it reduc on high heat, stirring with a wooden spoon until it has almost evaporated. Add th remaining butter or margarine, and pour ove the saltimbocca. Serve immediately, garnishe with tiny whole potatoes tossed in butter.

Veal Escalopes in Piquant Sauce

Trim 8 small veal escalopes (about $1\frac{1}{4}$ lb/600 g) beat, and dip in flour. Brown on all side over high heat in 3 oz (90 g) butter c margarine. Sprinkle with salt and arrange th escalopes on a warm serving dish. Prepare a sauce with 8 anchovy fillets, desalted an mashed with 1 tablespoon capers, choppe parsley, and a little oil and vinegar. Pour th sauce over the escalopes.

Sautéed Veal Escalopes

Trim 8 small veal escalopes (about $1\frac{1}{4}$ lb/600 g and beat well. Dip them in flour, and brown o all sides over high heat, in 3 oz (90 g) butter o margarine. Season with salt and pepper t taste, add a little stock, lower the heat an continue cooking for about 15 minute Arrange the meat on a serving dish and kee warm. Remove the pan from the heat, ad 2 egg yolks and the juice of 1 lemon, stir we and pour over the meat.

1

2

3

2

3

Viener Schnitzel

gredients: *4 large veal escalopes (about 1 lb/)0 g) · salt · pepper · flour · 1 egg · eadcrumbs · 3 oz (90 g) butter or argarine · 4 lemon slices · 2 olives · anchovy fillets · 1 tablespoon capers*

garnish: *hard-boiled eggs · parsley*

im the veal and beat well, season with salt d pepper to taste, dip lightly in flour, then in eaten egg (step 1), and in breadcrumbs, essing well to make them adhere. Brown the calopes, a few minutes on each side, over gh heat, in butter or margarine (step 2). rrange them on a warm serving dish, itting in the centre of each 1 peeled lemon ce, 1 anchovy fillet, desalted, rolled around pitted olive, and a few capers (step 3). arnish the edges of the dish with hard-iled egg slices and spigs of parsley and serve mediately.

Veal Cutlets with Sweetbread Stuffing

To prepare the stuffing lightly sauté 4 oz (115 g) sweetbreads and 4 oz (115 g) veal in 2 oz (60 g) butter mixed with chopped parsley and onion. Chop these ingredients and mash them in a mortar (or work them through a sieve) with 1 handful white bread, soaked in stock and squeezed dry. Add 1–2 eggs, 2 tablespoons grated Parmesan cheese, salt and pepper to taste, and mix well. The proportions can be adjusted according to the size of the cutlets. Beat 4 veal cutlets (with bone), season with salt and pepper to taste, and spread the stuffing on both sides of each cutlet.

Dip in beaten egg and in breadcrumbs, and fry in hot oil, or, if preferred, in oil and butter until cooked through. Drain well and serve immediately, garnished with parsley and with lemon quarters.

Veal Cutlets Bolognese

Trim the bone off 4 veal cutlets, beat them lightly, season with salt and pepper to taste, dip in flour, then in beaten egg, and finally in breadcrumbs, pressing well to make them adhere. Let them stand for $\frac{1}{2}$ hour, then brown on all sides over high heat in 3 oz (90 g) butter or margarine. Arrange them in a roasting pan, put on each 1 slice prosciutto, sprinkle with grated Parmesan cheese, dot with butter and put in a very hot oven (475°F/gas 9) for 2 minutes. Transfer to a warm serving dish, add a few tablespoons of gravy from a roast, or meat extract diluted in hot water, to the cooking juices, and pour over the cutlets.

Cutlets Valdostana Style are also made in this way but fontina (or Gruyère) cheese slices are used instead of Parmesan cheese.

1

2

3

Veal Pie with Marrow and Chicken Livers

Ingredients: *6 veal escalopes (about $1\frac{1}{4}$ lb/ 600 g), trimmed and well beaten* · *$\frac{1}{2}$ lb (225 g) marrow* · *4 oz (115 g) chicken livers* · *$\frac{1}{2}$ glass brandy* · *$\frac{1}{2}$ lb (225 g) sliced cooked ham* · *1 slice mortadella (4 oz/115 g)* · *2 egg yolks* · *4 oz (225 g) grated Parmesan cheese* · *8 fl oz (200 ml) cream* · *salt* · *pepper* · *grated nutmeg* · *butter or margarine* · *4–6 slices prosciutto*

To garnish: *green peas*

Scald the marrow in boiling water for a few minutes (step 1). Slice it, and slice the chicken livers. Sauté both in 1 oz (30 g) butter for a few minutes, add the brandy, flame it, remove from the heat and let cool. Add the chopped ham and mortadella, the egg yolks, Parmesan cheese, enough cream to obtain a soft mixture, and salt, pepper and nutmeg to taste. Grease a 7 × 3-inch mould with butter or margarine, and line it with prosciutto slices (step 2). Put 2 veal escalopes at the bottom of the mould, spread $\frac{1}{2}$ the stuffing over (step 3), repeat the layers, finishing with a layer of meat (i.e. 3 layers of meat and 2 of stuffing). Put over the whole the remaining slices of prosciutto. Bake in a moderate oven (350°F/gas 4) for about 1 hour. If, during the cooking, the prosciutto becomes too dry, cover with aluminium foil. Let the pie stand for 5 minutes before turning out onto a warm serving dish. Strain the cooking juices, reduce on high heat if necessary, and serve separately. Garnish the dish with buttered green peas. Serves 4–6.

Ligurian Meat Pie

Prepare a mushroom sauce as follows: so 1 tablespoon dried mushrooms in lukewar water, squeeze dry, chop roughly, and put a pan with 1 clove of garlic, peeled, 1 glass o 1 tablespoon chopped capers, and chopp parsley to taste. Let the mixture simmer for few minutes, then take from the heat, remo the garlic, and let cool. Using in all $1\frac{1}{2}$ (750 g) sliced veal or beef, put a layer of me (about $\frac{1}{2}$ lb/225 g) at the bottom of a hig narrow buttered pan. Cover with a layer mushroom sauce, then a layer of thin slices salt pork. Repeat the layers, ending with layer of veal or beef. Put over it a weight plate or cover. Cook slowly for about $1\frac{1}{4}$ hou

ork

oast Pork

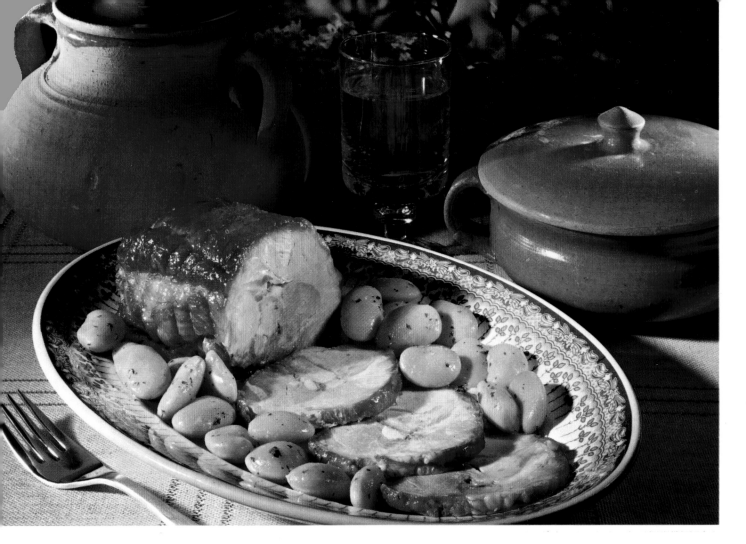

redients: *2 lb (1 kg) pork loin, boned and ed · 2 cloves of garlic · rosemary · 2–3 es · salt · freshly ground pepper · olive oil*

garnish: *tiny whole potatoes*

d the meat with halved or quartered cloves garlic (step 1), rosemary and cloves. Tie it h string, season with salt and pepper to te (step 2), brush with oil, and put it into an d roasting pan. Place in a hot oven (400°F/ 6) and roast for at least $1\frac{1}{2}$ hours, or until meat is cooked through and the juices are no longer pink, turning it over occasionally with 2 spoons and basting with the cooking juices. Untie it (step 3), let stand 5–10 minutes, and slice. Arrange the slices on a warm serving dish, garnished with tiny whole potatoes, boiled, tossed in butter and sprinkled with chopped parsley, and other vegetables according to taste. The dish is equally good when served cold. Serves 6.

Roast Pork with Orange Sauce

Tie 2 lb (1 kg) boned pork loin with string (see p.36). Season with salt and pepper to taste. Place in a buttered roasting pan with 1 slice onion and 1 celery stalk, cut into thin slices, 1 peeled orange in sections, 1 glass orange juice, and 1 tablespoon vinegar or 2 tablespoons dry white wine. Put the pan into a hot oven (400°F/gas 6) and cook for at least $1\frac{1}{2}$ hours, until the meat is cooked through, turning it and basting occasionally with the cooking juices. Remove meat from the pan, let stand 5–10 minutes, then slice it and place on a warm serving dish. Serve cooking juices separately.

Pork Loin with Piquant Sauce

Roll in flour 1 piece pork loin (about 2 lb/1 kg). Melt in a pan 2 oz (60 g) butter or margarine with chopped onion and capers to taste. Add the meat, brown on all sides over high heat, cover, lower the heat and cook very slowly for at least $1\frac{1}{2}$ hours, until the meat is cooked through, turning and adding stock occasionally. Add salt halfway through the cooking. When cooked, remove meat from the pan, let stand 5–10 minutes, then slice and arrange on a warm serving dish with the cooking juices and the juice of 1 lemon poured over. Sprinkle with capers. Serves 4–6.

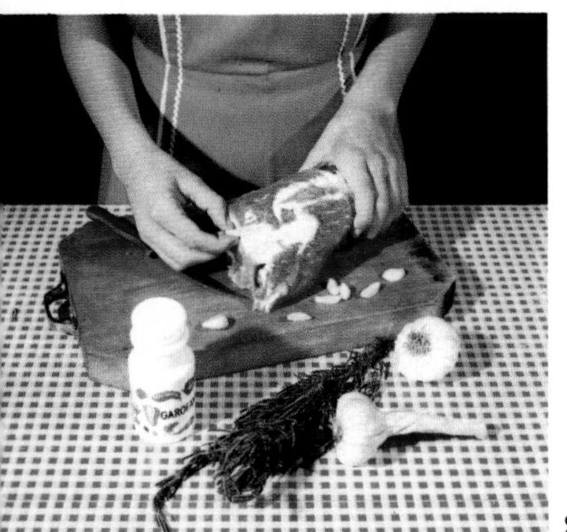

2

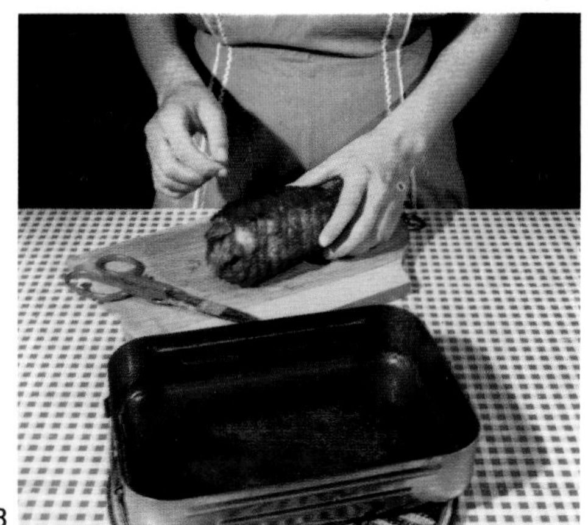

3

Crown Roast of Pork

Ingredients: *One 9-rib piece of pork* (carré)

For the stuffing: *4 oz (225 g) prosciutto or mortadella, chopped · 1 egg · 1 handful white bread, soaked in milk and squeezed dry · a few tablespoons Parmesan cheese · 1 tablespoon French mustard and 1 teaspoon Worcestershire sauce (optional) · chopped parsley · salt · pepper · oil*

To garnish: *tomatoes*

Prepare the *carré* by stripping the meat fro the upper part of the bones, and makir incisions in the meat between the low pieces of bone (step 1), or ask the butcher prepare it. Remove a little meat from th inside and chop it. Shape the ribs into a crow and tie it with string (step 2). Prepare th stuffing in the following manner: mix th chopped pork with the prosciutto, egg, brea Parmesan cheese, mustard, Worcestershi sauce (if using), parsley, and salt and pepper taste. Put the mixture, thoroughly blende inside the crown, and place in an oiled roasti pan. Brush it with oil (step 3) and cap the bo ends with aluminium foil. Place in a h oven (400°F/gas 6) and cook for at least hours, until the meat is cooked throug basting occasionally with the cooking juic The crown may be filled, if liked, with sm potatoes, fried in butter. Garnish with pap frills and tomatoes. Serves 6.

Roast Pork with Prunes

Soak 12 prunes in cold water overnight. Dra Take 1½ lb (750 g) pork tenderloin – or a other boneless cut suitable for roasting – a make a deep incision lengthwise into Insert the pitted prunes with a wooden spo handle. Brown the meat on all sides over hi heat in 1 oz (30 g) butter or margarir season with salt to taste, add some stock, cov lower the heat, and cook for about 1 ho turning and basting occasionally with t cooking juices, adding more stock if the me becomes too dry.

The cooking can also be done in the ov at 350°F/gas 4. Halfway through the cooki add 4 apples, peeled and cored, with a pat butter in the centre.

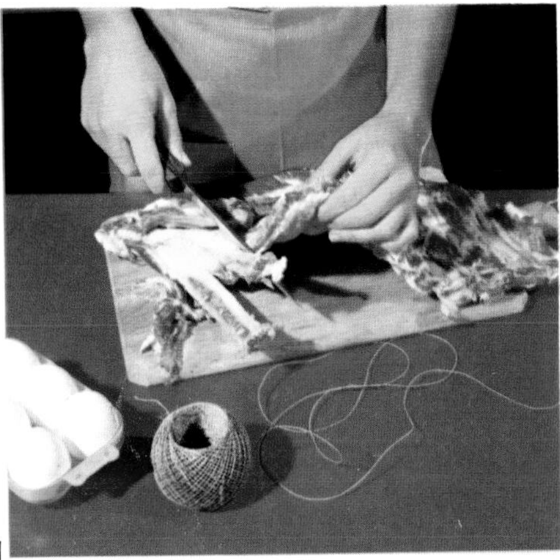
1

2

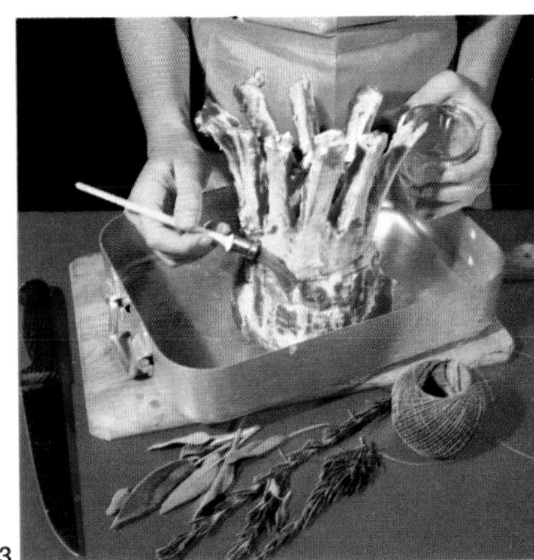
3

2

3

pare Ribs Stew

gredients: *$1\frac{1}{4}$ lb (600 g) spare ribs · z (115 g) pork rind · 1 pig's trotter · nion · 2 oz (60 g) salt pork · 1 oz) g) butter · 3 celery stalks · 2–3 carrots · ablespoons tomato sauce · salt · pepper · b (750 g) cabbage · $\frac{3}{4}$ lb (340 g) sausages*

rape and scorch the rind and the pig's trotter. lve the trotter lengthwise, and cook in boil- water for $\frac{1}{2}$ hour, skimming most of the fat. ain and cut into pieces. Chop the onion d salt pork, and brown in butter. Add the tter, rind, and spare ribs also cut into pieces ep 1). When browned, add the celery and rrots, roughly chopped (step 2), the tomato uce diluted in a little hot water, and salt and pper to taste. After a few minutes add ough water to cover. Cover the pan, and ok slowly for $2\frac{1}{2}$–3 hours. Separate the bage leaves, wash, and put in a pan of iling water. Drain after 10 minutes. Half hour before the cooking is complete, add cabbage (step 3), and the sausage cut into pieces. The cooking juices must be thoroughly reduced before the dish is served.

Sauerkraut with Frankfurters

Wash thoroughly 3 lb ($1\frac{1}{2}$ kg) sauerkraut, drain and squeeze to remove all water. Put in a pan with plenty of water $\frac{1}{2}$ lb (225 g) smoked bacon, $\frac{1}{2}$ calf's foot and 6 oz (175 g) pork rind. Bring to the boil, then drain. Line the bottom of a pan with the pork rind, put in half the sauerkraut, the bacon, $\frac{1}{2}$ lb (225 g) smoked pork shoulder, the calf's foot, 6 frankfurters, 1 garlic sausage, 1 carrot, 1 small onion stuck with 1 clove, 10 juniper berries, 1 bouquet garni, made of parsley, thyme and 1 bay leaf, salt, 3 oz (90 g) butter or margarine, and the remaining sauerkraut. Add 1 cup dry white wine, and enough water to cover. Seal the pan with a double sheet of wax paper or aluminium foil, and cook very slowly for about $2\frac{1}{2}$ hours. After $\frac{1}{2}$ hour remove the sausage and the frankfurters and keep on one side, and after $1\frac{1}{2}$ hours, remove the pork shoulder and the bacon. Add $\frac{3}{4}$ lb (340 g) peeled potatoes, and continue cooking for $\frac{1}{2}$ hour. Put back everything to reheat for 10 minutes. By the end of the cooking, the liquid must be almost completely absorbed. The calf's foot is used only to give consistency to the stock and is not served with the sauerkraut, but it can be boned, cut into strips, and served separately, seasoned with oil, vinegar, and raw onion slices, if liked. Serves 4–6.

1

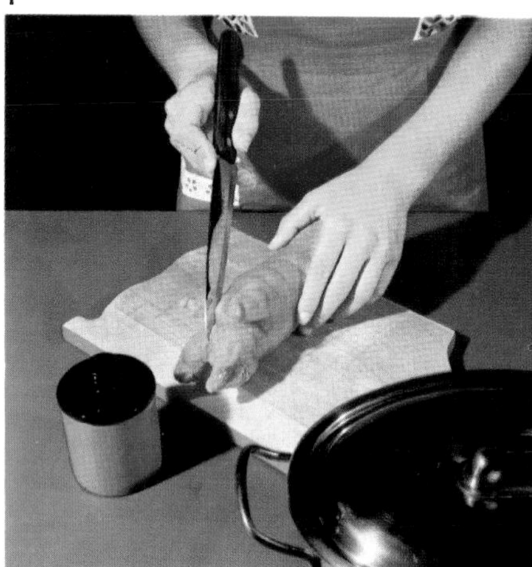

2

3

Stuffed Pig's Trotter with Lentils

Ingredients: *1 pig's trotter (about 2 lb/1 kg) · 1 lb (500 g) lentils · 2 oz (60 g) salt pork · $\frac{3}{4}$ lb (340 g) sausage meat · 2 celery stalks · 1 carrot, peeled · 2 onions, peeled · 1 oz (30 g) butter or margarine · stock · tomato sauce (optional) · salt · pepper*

Soak the pig's trotter and the lentils separately in cold water for 24 hours. Remove the pig's trotter from the water (reserving the water), prick with a trussing needle (step 1), or a fork, and make small incisions near the nails (step 2). Wrap it in a cloth (step 3), and tie with string. Put it in a pan with the reserved soaking water and bring to a boil. Lower the heat and cook slowly for $3\frac{1}{2}$ hours. Soak the salt pork in cold water for 1 hour. Remove the pig's trotter from the heat and let it stand in the cooking liquid for 30 minutes. Remove from pan, bone carefully and stuff with the sausage meat. Tie with string, return to pan and cook until tender together with 1 celery stalk, the carrot and 1 onion. Drain the lentils. In the butter or margarine sauté the salt pork and remaining onion and celery, chopped together. Add the lentils with a little stock and tomato sauce, if using. Cover and cook slowly until all the liquid is absorbed. Serve the stuffed pig's trotter sliced with the lentils and with cabbage.

Rolled Garlic Sausage

Beat thoroughly $1\frac{1}{4}$ lb (600 g) beef or veal in the slice. Cover it with a layer of spinach – fresh or frozen – lightly sautéed in butter with a little garlic. Place a skinned $\frac{3}{4}$-lb (340-g) garlic sausage in the centre, roll the meat lengthwise and tie it with string. Brown the meat on sides over high heat in 2 oz (60 g) butter, a $\frac{1}{2}$ glass dry white wine, let it reduce, seas with salt to taste, and add some stock. Cov lower the heat and cook for 2 hours, addi more stock if the meat becomes dry. Let t roll stand for 10 minutes, slice and serve w the reduced cooking juices.

Sausage Hotpot

Sauté a little chopped onion in 1 oz (30 butter or margarine. Add 8 sausages (skinn or not, according to taste) and brown the Add 2 tablespoons tomato paste diluted in little hot water, or 6 oz (175 g) peeled tomat worked through a sieve and 1 bay leaf. Cov and cook slowly for about $\frac{1}{2}$ hour. Serve w mashed potato or polenta.

ffal

weetbreads with lushrooms

gredients: *1¼ lb (600 g) veal sweetbreads · non juice or vinegar · pinch of salt · flour · lb (500 g) fresh mushrooms · 2 oz (60 g) tter · ½ small glass brandy · stock · uble cream*

finish: *1 egg yolk · juice of ½ lemon · opped parsley · whole button mushrooms ptional)*

ak the sweetbreads in cold salted water for hours with a little lemon juice or vinegar. nse them, put them in a pan, and cover with ld water. Add salt and more lemon juice vinegar. Bring to the boil and cook for 5 minutes, skimming occasionally. Take out the sweetbreads, drain, and rinse again in fresh cold water. Remove the fat, skin and ducts, and let the sweetbreads cool. Slice them (step 1), roll lightly in flour, and brown them on all sides over high heat in the butter. Add the brandy and flame it. Add the mushrooms cut into thin slices (step 2), and, after a moment, add the stock. Lower the heat and cook slowly for 25 minutes. Add the cream, let it thicken on very low heat, then turn off the heat. Add the egg yolk beaten with the lemon juice (step 3), and serve as soon as it has blended with the other ingredients. Sprinkle with chopped parsley, garnish with sprigs of parsley and serve with whole button mushrooms, if liked.

Paupiettes of Brains

Soak 1 lb (500 g) calf's brains in cold salted water, with the juice of ½ lemon for 2–3 hours. Drain. Cover the brains in stock or water, and simmer for 10–15 minutes until firm, then take them out, drain, and rinse under cold running water. Remove the skins. Dry the brains and let cool. Chop finely and mix with 2 beaten eggs, 2 tablespoons grated Parmesan cheese, and chopped parsley, salt, pepper and grated nutmeg to taste.

Brown the mixture, 1 spoonful at a time, on all sides in melted butter. Serve on a warm dish garnished with parsley sprigs and lemon quarters.

Beef Marrow Paupiettes

Soak 1 lb (500 g) beef marrow in cold water for 1 hour, drain, and cook in boiling water for 10 minutes. Season with salt towards the end of the cooking. Drain, rinse under cold running water, remove the skins, dry and let cool. Sauté in butter and cut carefully into 3-inch pieces.

Place each piece on 1 slice ham with 2 white truffle slices, and roll the ham. Tie each paupiette with string. Dip in beaten egg and breadcrumbs, and brown them on all sides in golden butter.

2

3

Stuffed Veal Heart

Ingredients: *1 veal heart (about 2 lb/1 kg) · 2 oz (60 g) butter or margarine · 1 onion, sliced · 10 oz (300 g) carrots, sliced · 1 bouquet garni, made of parsley, celery, sage and 1 bay leaf · $\frac{1}{2}$ glass dry white wine*

For the stuffing: *4 oz (115 g) pork loin, choppe or sausage meat · $\frac{1}{2}$ onion · 1 clove of garlic · parsley · 1 egg · 2 tablespoons grated Parmesan cheese · salt · pepper*

To prepare the stuffing: mix the chopped por loin or sausage meat with the $\frac{1}{2}$ onion, garli and parsley, all chopped, the egg, the grate Parmesan cheese, and salt and pepper t taste (step 1). Trim the heart with scissors cutting the wall dividing the interior. Soak i salted water for 1 hour, and dry. Put in th prepared stuffing (step 2), and sew up th opening with string (step 3). Brown in th butter or margarine. Add the sliced onion an carrot, bouquet garni, wine, and salt an pepper to taste. Cover, and cook on moderat heat for $1\frac{1}{2}$ hours, or until tender. Serve th sliced heart with the cooking juices.

Veal Kidneys Bolognese

Skin 4 veal kidneys, slice them lengthwis and remove the core. Soak them for 1 hou in water mixed with a little vinegar. Drain dry, and cut into slices. Brown in 2 oz (60 g butter or margarine some parsley and onion finely chopped, add the kidney slices and le them brown. Add salt and pepper to taste $1\frac{1}{2}$ tablespoons vinegar, a few tablespoons stoc to cover, and continue cooking for a furthe 10 minutes, until kidneys are tender. Serv immediately.

Veal Kidneys with Capers

Prepare and slice 4 veal kidneys, as above Roll the slices in flour, season with salt an pepper to taste, and brown then on high hea in 2 oz (60 g) butter or margarine. Add glass dry white wine, let it reduce, and ad 1 tablespoon capers, chopped if large, whol if small. Mix well, continue cooking for 10 o more minutes until kidneys are tender. Serv immediately, sprinkled with chopped parsley if liked.

1

2

3

:alf's Liver with Onions

ıgredients: *1¼ lb (600 g) calf's liver, thinly iced · 2 large onions · 4 oz (115 g) butter · ılt · pepper · flour*

ɔ serve: *lemon quarters*

ıt the onions into thin slices (step 1). Cook em very slowly in half the butter until ɔlden-brown. Season with salt and pepper to ste. Roll the liver slices lightly in flour tep 2). Brown them quickly in the remaining ıtter in a separate pan, and continue cooking r just a few minutes. Remove from the heat, ɔrinkle with salt, place on a warm serving sh, arrange the onions around them, and ɛrve immediately with lemon quarters. Calf's ver Venetian Style is prepared in a slightly different way: the onions should be cut into somewhat thicker slices and browned in oil on high heat. The liver, cut into small slices or strips, should be put in the same pan as the onions. After 2 or 3 minutes, season with salt and pepper and serve with lemon quarters.

Braised Calf's Liver with Sage

Lard 1¼ lb (600 g) calf's liver with 4 oz (115 g) finely diced salt pork (soaked in cold water for 1 hour and drained). Brown lightly, in a high, narrow pan, 2 oz (60 g) butter or margarine together with 15 sage leaves, add the liver and sauté it quickly on all sides. Sprinkle with salt, and cover with stock. Cover, and cook slowly for about 2 hours. Ten minutes before the cooking is completed, add 1 glass milk, and reduce the juices on high heat. Serve the sliced liver with the cooking juices strained through a sieve, accompanied by mashed potatoes.

Calf's Liver with Red Wine

Cut into thin slices 1¼ lb (600 g) calf's liver. Roll the slices in flour, and brown them quickly in 2 oz (60 g) butter. Add 1 tablespoon grated onion, cook for 1–2 minutes but do not brown, add 1 glass good red wine, and boil for a few minutes. Blend in a knob of butter, season with salt to taste, then remove the liver slices and arrange them on a warm serving dish. Pour over the cooking juice, and sprinkle with chopped parsley.

2

3

1

2

3

Calf's Tongue with Olives

Ingredients: *2 calves' tongues, about 2 lb (1 kg) · chopped onion, garlic and parsley · 3 oz (90 g) butter or margarine · about $\frac{1}{2}$ lb (225 g) medium-sized green olives · stock · salt · pepper*

Bring the tongues to a boil in water, rinse under cold running water and drain. Simmer in enough water to cover for $1\frac{1}{2}$–2 hours until tender, then skin (step 1) and slice. Melt the buttér, and sauté on low heat the chopped onion, garlic and parsley, together with the olives, pitted or whole according to taste (step 2). Add the tongue slices (step 3) and $1\frac{1}{2}$ tablespoons stock and continue cooking until the tongue is well heated and has absorbed much of the flavour of the other ingredients.

Transfer to a warm serving dish and serve the tongue with the cooking juices, surrounded by the olives.

Braised Beef Tongue

Cook 1 beef tongue (about 5 lb/$2\frac{1}{2}$ kg) in salted boiling water for $\frac{1}{2}$ hour. Drain and skin. Roll strips of bacon or salt pork (soaked in cold water for 1 hour and drained) in a mixture of chopped garlic, parsley, salt and pepper to taste. Lard the tongue with them. Roll the tongue lightly in flour. Brown in a large shallow pan 2 oz (60 g) butter or margarine. Add the tongue, 2 onions and 2 carrots, thinly sliced. Skim the fat, then add 1 cup dry white wine, and let it reduce by half. Add $\frac{1}{2}$ cup stock, 1 bouquet garni made of parsley, thyme, celery and 1 bay leaf, and salt and pepper to taste. Cover, and continue cooking very slowly for $2\frac{1}{2}$–3 hours until very tender, adding more stock as necessary – the juices must be thick and not fatty. Serve the tongue with the cooking juices poured over. Serves 8–10.

Calf's Tongue with Spring Onions

Bring 2 calves' tongues (about $1\frac{3}{4}$ lb/900 g) to boil in salted water, rinse under cold runnir water and drain. Simmer in enough water cover for $1\frac{1}{2}$–2 hours until tender. Skin ther dry, and roll lightly in flour. Sauté 1 slice onion in 2 oz (60 g) butter. Add the tongue an brown it. Add $\frac{1}{2}$ glass dry white wine, let reduce, add $\frac{1}{2}$ lb (225 g) peeled tomatoes or tablespoon tomato paste diluted in a little stoc Add $\frac{1}{2}$ cup hot stock, cover, and continu cooking for 15 minutes. Meanwhile, soak 1 (500 g) spring onions in boiling water. Pe them, put them in the pan, and continue cook ing until the tongue has absorbed the flavou of the cooking juices. Slice the tongue an serve with the reduced cooking juices, gar nished with the spring onions.

3raised Tripe with Spanish Beans

ıgredients: *2 lb (1 kg) honeycomb tripe · ilk · salt · $\frac{1}{2}$ lb (225 g) dry white Spanish ·ans · 6 oz (175 g) butter · 1 oz (30 g) salt ırk, soaked in cold water for 1 hour and ·ained · chopped celery, carrot, onion, garlic and ıge, to taste · $\frac{1}{2}$ glass dry white wine · 0 oz (300 g) canned peeled tomatoes, sieved · bay leaf · pepper · mixed herbs · stock · ·ated Parmesan cheese (optional)*

ɔak the beans in cold water for at least 12 ours. Put them in cold water without salt, ring to the boil, and cook until tender. Cook the ·ipe in a mixture of milk and water to cover nd a pinch of salt for 1 hour. Drain. Cut into :rips (step 1). Brown the butter together with ıe salt pork and chopped vegetables (step 2). dd the tripe and, after 1–2 minutes, the ·hite wine. Let it reduce, add the tomatoes, ıe bay leaf, and salt, pepper and mixed herbs to taste, and cook for about $1\frac{1}{2}$ hours, adding stock occasionally if the tripe becomes dry. Fifteen minutes before the end of the cooking, add the drained beans (step 3). Before serving the tripe, together with the reduced juices, add grated Parmesan cheese, if desired.

Tripe Creole

Cook 2 lb (1 kg) tripe as above, and cut into strips. Brown 2 oz (60 g) butter or margarine together with 1 large chopped onion. Add 1 oz (30 g) chopped salt pork, soaked in water for 1 hour and drained, 1 clove of garlic, chopped, 1 bay leaf, and, after a few minutes, $\frac{3}{4}$ lb (340 g) tomatoes, peeled and chopped, 2 green peppers, cut into strips, the tripe, and a little salt and pepper to taste.

Cover and cook slowly for about $1\frac{1}{4}$ hours, adding stock if the tripe becomes dry.

Braised Tripe with Potatoes

Cook 2 lb (1 kg) tripe as above, and cut into strips. Brown in 3 oz (90 g) butter or margarine a chopped mixture of garlic, onion, carrot and rosemary to taste, and 2 green olives. Add the tripe and, after a few minutes, 2–3 tablespoons tomato paste diluted in a little stock, or 6 oz (175 g) canned peeled tomatoes passed through a sieve, and a pinch of grated nutmeg. Cover, and cook on very low heat for $\frac{3}{4}$ hour. Add $1\frac{1}{4}$ lb (600 g) potatoes, cut into pieces, stock, and cook for a further 30–45 minutes.

2

3

Lamb

Stuffed Shoulder of Lamb

Ingredients: *1 shoulder of lamb (about 2 lb/ 1 kg) · 4 oz (115 g) salt pork (soaked in cold water for 1 hour and drained), or prosciutto · a generous measure of fresh rosemary, parsley and a few celery leaves · 1 clove of garlic, peeled (optional) · salt · pepper · 2 oz (60 g) butter or margarine · ½ glass dry white wine · stock*

To garnish: *macedoine of mixed vegetables*

Chop the salt pork or prosciutto together with the rosemary, parsley, celery and garlic (if using). Season with salt and pepper to taste. Bone the shoulder of lamb (step 1), or ask your butcher to do it for you. Beat it until as flat as possible, and cover the inside with the chopped mixture (step 2), roll it and tie with string (step 3). Brown it on all sides over high heat in the butter or margarine, and sprinkle with salt. Add the white wine, let it reduce, then add some stock. Cover, lower the heat, and cook for about 1½ hours until tender, adding more stock if the meat becomes dry. Remove from the pan, let stand for 10 minutes, then remove string and slice the meat. Arrange on a warm serving dish with the cooking juices. Garnish with a macedoine of mixed vegetables.

Carré d'Agneau

Have the butcher prepare a *carré* of lamb with best end of neck cutlets, cutting through the base of each cutlet without completely separating them. Brown over high heat in 2 oz (60 g) butter or margarine on top of the stove, then put it in a wide buttered ovenproof dish. Season with salt and pepper to taste, and put the *carré* in a hot oven (400°F/gas 6). Cook for at least 1 hour until the meat is tender, turning it once. Prepare a mixture of parsley, mint and garlic, chopped, breadcrumbs, and salt and pepper to taste. Spread it over the fatty parts of the lamb, pressing to make it adhere. Pour over melted butter and gratiné.

Lamb Cutlets with Mashed Potatoes

Prepare mashed potatoes according to taste with 2 lb (1 kg) potatoes, butter, milk, salt and grated nutmeg. Brown 8 lamb cutlets in 2 oz (60 g) butter or margarine on both sides over high heat, and cook for 7–8 minutes, turnin once. Season with salt and pepper to tast Drain the cutlets and keep warm. In the f remaining in the pan, brown 4 slices prosciutt or bacon. Arrange the cutlets and the prosciutt or bacon over the potatoes and pour over th cooking juices.

1

2

3

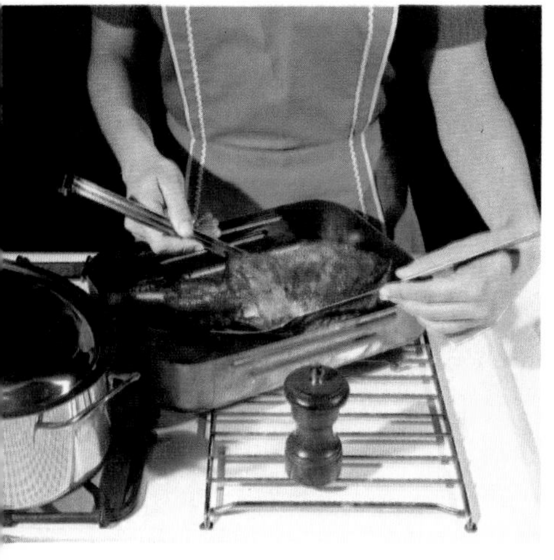

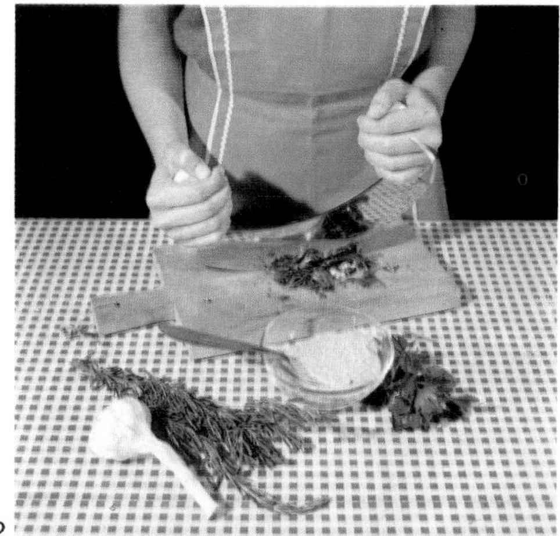

2

3

Roast Lamb

Ingredients: *1 leg of lamb (about 3 lb/$1\frac{1}{2}$ kg) · 2 oz (60 g) butter or margarine · garlic, rosemary and parsley · a few tablespoons breadcrumbs · salt · pepper*

In an ovenproof casserole brown the leg of lamb in $\frac{3}{4}$ of the butter or margarine on all sides over high heat. Season with salt and pepper to taste and add the remaining butter or margarine. Put it in a hot oven (400°F/gas 6) and cook for about 1 hour 20 minutes or until tender (step 1). Chop the garlic, rosemary and parsley, and mix with the breadcrumbs (step 2). Spread the mixture over the meat (step 3), and continue cooking for 5–10 minutes, in the top of the oven, until a golden crust has formed.

Braised Lamb

Cut into pieces 3 lb ($1\frac{1}{2}$ kg) lamb meat (neck, shoulder, etc.). Roll the pieces in flour, and brown them on all sides over high heat in 2 oz (60 g) butter or margarine. Add $\frac{1}{2}$ glass dry white wine, let it reduce, then add 1 crushed clove of garlic, 1 large onion and 1 carrot cut into slices, 1 clove and 1 bouquet garni. After 2 minutes add 2 tablespoons tomato paste diluted in 1 cup water. Season with salt and pepper to taste, cover, lower the heat and cook slowly for about 1 hour or until the meat is tender. Remove the bouquet garni and the garlic before serving.

Lamb Paupiettes

Mince 1 lb (500 g) boned lamb shoulder. Mix it with 1–2 handfuls white bread soaked in milk and squeezed dry, 2–3 tablespoons grated Parmesan or Gruyère cheese, 1 egg, and salt and pepper to taste. Blend well, shape into a ball and beat repeatedly against the bottom of the bowl. Make 4 flat paupiettes – or 8 smaller ones – and roll them in flour. Brown them on all sides over high heat in 1 oz (30 g) butter or margarine and cook for about 30 minutes, turning them once. Serve a tomato sauce separately.

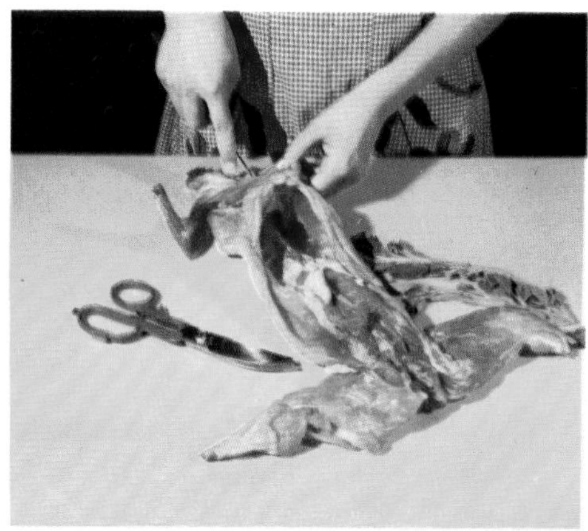

1

2

3

Rabbit

Stuffed Boned Rabbit

Ingredients: *1 rabbit (about 4 lb/2 kg) · a generous measure rosemary and sage · salt · pepper · 6 oz (175 g) prosciutto (sliced), or salt pork (soaked in cold water for 1 hour, drained and sliced) · 1 clove of garlic, peeled · 2 oz (60 g) butter · 2 tablespoons oil · 2 glasses dry white wine · stock*

To garnish: *macedoine of vegetables*

Wash and dry the rabbit. Place it on its back on a cutting board with the neck towards you, and make a cut lengthwise along the breast and belly (step 1). Using a very sharp knife carefully remove all the bones (step 2), so as to obtain 1 large piece of meat. Mix the rosemary and sage with salt and pepper to taste, spread $\frac{1}{2}$ the mixture over the meat, arrange a layer of prosciutto or salt pork slices over it, and top with the remainder of the herb mixture. Roll the meat (step 3), tie it with string as for any roast meat. Sauté the garlic in the oil and butter until golden, add the meat and brown on all sides over high heat. Remove the garlic. Stir in the white wine, let it reduce, then add salt to taste and some stock. Lower the heat and cook slowly for $1\frac{1}{4}$ hours. When cooked, remove the roll from the pan, let stand 10 minutes, then remove the string, slice the meat and arrange on a warm serving dish with the reduced cooking juices poured over. Garnish the dish with a macedoine of vegetables, if liked. The rabbit can also be cooked in a moderate oven (350°F/gas 4) for $1\frac{1}{2}$–2 hours, basting the meat occasionally with the cooking juices. Serves 6–8.

Rabbit with Curry Sauce

Wash and dry 1 rabbit (about 2 lb/1 kg). Cu into serving pieces, roll in flour, and brown o all sides over high heat in 2 oz (60 g) butte In another pan, sauté until golden 1 clove c garlic, peeled, in 3 oz (90 g) butter. Remov the garlic, add 1 medium-sized green appl cored and roughly chopped, 1 medium-size onion, finely chopped, and $\frac{1}{2}$ teaspoon curr powder – or more, according to taste. Coo slowly until the onion is tender, then add tablespoons flour, and salt to taste. Stir con stantly, and after 2 minutes, add 16 fl o (460 ml) hot stock. Add the pieces of rabbi cover, lower the heat and cook slowly for 40-45 minutes or until tender. Serve with th cooking juices poured over, and boiled rice o pilaff in a separate dish, if liked.

2

3

ᵓoultry

oiled Stuffed Capon

gredients: *1 capon (about 5 lb/$2\frac{1}{2}$ kg) ·*
celery stick · 1 leek · 1 potato ·
lb (225 g) small onions, peeled and halved ·
carrot · stock

r the stuffing: *2 oz (60 g) butter or*
argarine · the capon's liver, finely chopped ·
oz (60 g) boned pork loin, finely chopped ·
oz (60 g) prosciutto, finely chopped ·
oz (60 g) sweetbreads or brains (see p.39),
tional · 1 handful white bread, soaked in milk
d squeezed dry · parsley or truffles ·
egg yolks · grated Parmesan cheese · salt ·
pper · grated nutmeg

Wash and dry the capon (step 1). If you like, remove the bones from inside the breast, taking care not to spoil the shape of the bird. Peel the vegetables and cut into pieces if large.

Prepare the stuffing: sauté lightly in the butter or margarine the capon's liver, pork loin, prosciutto, and the sweetbreads or brains, if using. Add the bread and parsley. (If truffles are used, cut them into thin slices and add them later to the chopped mixture.) Put the mixture in a bowl with the egg yolks, grated Parmesan cheese, and salt, pepper and nutmeg to taste, and blend thoroughly. Stuff the capon with the mixture, sew it with string (steps 2 and 3), wrap it in a clean napkin or cloth, and tie at both ends. Put it in a pan, cover with stock and bring slowly to the boil. Skim the scum, add the vegetables and continue cooking slowly for about 2 hours, or until the capon is tender. Remove it from the pan, take it out of the cloth, and let stand 10 minutes. Remove string, transfer meat to a warm serving dish, and surround with the vegetables from the cooking juices. Serve with a variety of sharp sauces, according to taste. If liked, the capon can be carved before serving and reshaped on the serving dish. Alternatively the stuffed capon can be roasted in a moderate oven (375°F/ gas 5) for 2 hours. Serves 6–8.

Capon with Chicken Livers and Mushrooms

Wash and dry a 5-lb ($2\frac{1}{2}$-kg) capon. Clean $\frac{3}{4}$ lb (340 g) mushrooms, chop them, and sauté for a few minutes in 1 oz (30 g) butter, together with 3 sliced chicken livers. Season with salt and pepper to taste, add 2 tablespoons hot brandy, bring to the boil and flame. Remove from the heat after a few minutes, and mix with 1 handful white bread, previously soaked in milk and squeezed dry, 1 egg yolk, grated Parmesan cheese and chopped parsley to taste. Stuff the capon and proceed as above.

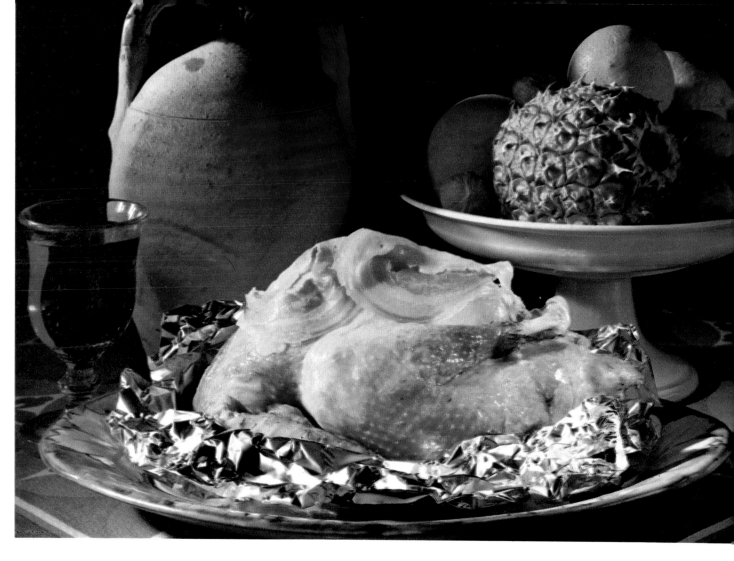

Chicken Cooked in Clay

Ingredients: *1 chicken (about 3 lb/1½ kg) · a finely chopped mixture of juniper berries, sage, 1 bay leaf, thyme and peppercorns · salt · 4 oz (115 g) salt pork (soaked in cold water for 1 hour, drained and sliced) or prosciutto slices*

Wash and dry the chicken, put inside it 1 teaspoon of the chopped mixture and salt (step 1), and tie it with string. Brush it with the remaining mixture, then cover with the salt pork or prosciutto slices. Wrap in aluminium foil, sealing it well. Soak the clay and work it thoroughly. Spread clay in a layer not less than ½ inch thick, and cover the wrapped bird on all sides with the clay (step 2). Put in a very hot oven (475°F/gas 9) until the clay begins to crack. Break the clay (step 3), remove the bird, and open the wrapping when you serve. The chicken can also be cooked in the aluminium foil, without the clay, in a hot oven (400°F/gas 6) for 1–1½ hours or until tender.

Chicken with Lentils

Soak in cold water for 12 hours 1 lb (500 g) lentils. Drain, put in cold water, and cook for 2 hours together with 1 clove of garlic, 1 celery stick and salt. Meanwhile prepare for cooking a 3-lb (1½ kg) chicken. Put inside it 1 bay leaf and salt and pepper to taste. Put on the bottom of a casserole 4 oz (115 g) butter or margarine in small pieces, some celery, carrot and onion, roughly chopped, some chopped ham fat, and ½ clove of garlic, peeled. Put in the chicken and brown very slowly. Sprinkle with plenty salt and pepper. Add ½ glass dry white wine, it reduce, then add a few ladles stock. Cover a continue cooking slowly for 1½ hours or u tender. Lift out the bird and keep it wa Drain the lentils, sauté them for a few minu in the chicken's cooking juices, and serve th with the carved bird.

Roast Chicken

Wash and dry a 3-lb (1½-kg) chicken. Ch sage, rosemary and garlic, and season it w plenty of salt and pepper. Put 1 tablespoon the mixture inside the chicken and roast in hot oven (400°F/gas 6) for about 1½ hou

1

2

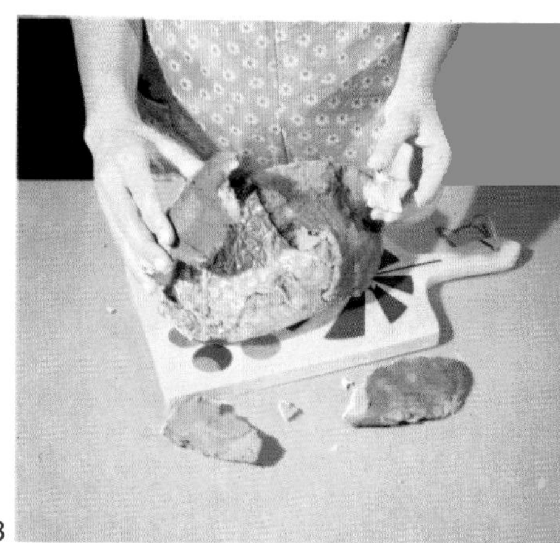

3

2

3

꞉oast Goose

ꞏ**gredients:** *1 goose (about 7 lb/3½ kg) · oz (60 g) butter or margarine · sage · ꞏsemary · salt · pepper · ½ glass dry white wine*

) garnish: *tiny whole potatoes, boiled · ꞏrsley sprigs*

'ash and dry the goose. Put inside it 1 table- ꞏoon butter or margarine mixed with chopped ꞏsemary and sage, and salt to taste (step 1). ꞏe with string and sprinkle the outside liber- ly with salt and pepper (step 2). Dot the ꞏose with the remaining butter or margarine, ace it in a roasting pan with more chopped ꞏsemary and sage to taste in a hot oven ꞏ75°F/gas 9). When brown, baste it with hite wine (step 3), lower the heat to moder- ꞏe (375°F/gas 5), and continue cooking for ꞏout 2 hours, pricking occasionally with a rk to let the fat escape. When the goose is ꞏoked, remove from the pan and let stand 10 minutes. Remove string, transfer to a warm serving dish, arrange paper frills on legs and garnish with tiny whole potatoes and parsley sprigs. (Half a goose can be roasted in the same way: place it in a lightly buttered roasting pan with the skin above so that it can be pricked occasionally.) Serves 6–8.

Stuffed Goose Neck

Detach the skin from the neck, turning it inside out without breaking it, wash, dry, and tie with string at one end. Soak the liver from the goose in tepid water for 1 hour, then drain and chop it. Sauté it in a little butter or margarine, together with the chopped goose heart, without letting them brown. Chop ½ lb (225g) raw pork loin. Mix liver, heart and pork with 4 oz (115 g) sausage meat, 1 handful white bread, soaked in milk and squeezed dry, 1 slice of onion (optional), chopped parsley to taste, 2 tablespoons brandy, and plenty of salt and pepper. Stuff the mixture into the neck skin, leaving a little space to provide for swelling during the cooking, and tie the other end. Roll it with the hand to make it regular, and prick it all over with a fine needle. Put it in cold stock, and cook it for about 1 hour. Slice it, and serve it hot with buttered spinach or mashed potatoes. Or you may serve it cold, possibly with aspic and a green salad.

An alternative way of cooking this dish is to brown the goose neck in goose fat and then braise it slowly with chopped celery, carrot, garlic, 1 bay leaf, and stock for about 1 hour.

Chicken Breasts with Cheese Cream

Ingredients: *4 chicken breasts (1 lb/500 g) · flour · salt · pepper · 2 oz (60 g) butter or margarine · dry white wine or brandy · stock*

For the Cheese Cream: *4 oz (115 g) cream cheese · 1 oz (30 g) butter · 1 tablespoon milk · pepper · truffles or black olives (optional) · peas*

Beat lightly the chicken breasts, season with salt and pepper to taste, flour them lightly, and cook them in the butter or margarine on both sides, on high heat, until golden (step 1). Add the white wine or brandy (if using brandy bring it to the boil and flame it), let it reduce then add immediately a few tablespoons stock and stir to combine all the cooking juices. Cover and cook slowly for 30–35 minutes.

To prepare the cheese cream, put in a pan the cheese (step 2), butter, milk, and pepper to taste and blend over low heat until creamy. Spread it over the chicken breasts (step 3), and put them under the grill to brown for a few seconds. Transfer to a warm serving dish and garnish with a few sliced truffles or pitted black olives, if liked, and serve with peas.

Chicken Breasts with Brandy

Melt 2 oz (60 g) butter in a pan. Put in, side by side, 4 chicken breasts (about 1 lb/500 g), lightly beaten and floured. Season with salt and pepper to taste. Brown them quickly on both sides, on high heat, then cover, lower the heat, and cook slowly for 30–35 minutes. When cooked, arrange them on a warm serving dish, covered with the cooking juices. Heat 1 small glass brandy, flame it, pour over the chicken breasts, and serve immediately.

Stuffed Chicken Breasts

Beat lightly 4 chicken breasts (about 1 lb/500 g), and put in the centre of each a stuffing prepared in the following manner: mix 3 oz (90 g) cottage or ricotta cheese with 1 egg yolk, 1 teaspoon chopped parsley, 1 teaspoon grated lemon peel, and salt and pepper to taste. Roll the meat and tie with string. Flour lightly and brown on all sides over high heat in 2 oz (60 g) butter or margarine. Season with salt and pepper to taste. Add 1 small glass brandy, heated, bring to a boil, flame it, let it reduce, then add some hot stock. Cover, lower the heat and cook slowly for about 30–35 minutes.

1

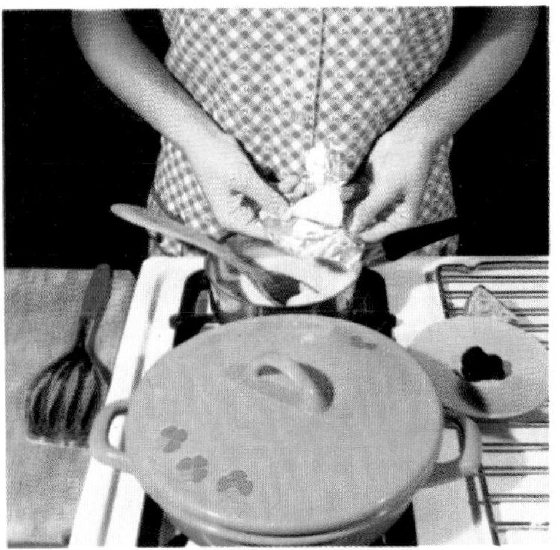
2

3

Stuffed Roast Pigeons

ngredients: *2 large pigeons · 4 slices salt ork, soaked in cold water for 1 hour and rained, or streaky bacon · 1 oz (30 g) butter · glass brandy · salt · 1 bay leaf · tock*

'or the stuffing: *1 oz (30 g) butter · ivers from the pigeons, minced · oz (60 g) prosciutto, diced · ½ glass brandy · handful white bread, soaked in milk and queezed dry · 1 egg yolk · tablespoons grated Parmesan cheese · hopped parsley · salt · pepper*

'o serve: *carrots in white sauce*

Vash and dry the pigeons, cutting off the feet step 1). Prepare the stuffing: sauté lightly in 1 z (30 g) butter the minced livers and prosiutto. Add ½ glass brandy, bring to the boil, ame it, and remove from the heat. Mix the vers and prosciutto with the bread, egg yolk, rated Parmesan cheese, and parsley, salt and epper to taste. Stuff the pigeons with the nixture and sew the openings with string. lace 2 slices salt pork or bacon on the breast f each bird (step 2), tie them with string, and rown on all sides over high heat in the remainig butter. Pour over the remaining brandy step 3), bring to the boil, flame it, sprinkle with alt, add the bay leaf, cover, lower the heat, nd cook for about 1 hour until tender, adding ock if the meat becomes dry. If the pigeons re small, allow 1 per person and double the uantity of stuffing ingredients. When cooked, emove the string, transfer to a warm serving ish and serve surrounded by carrots in a hite sauce.

igeons with Mushrooms

Vash and dry 2 large pigeons (or 4 small ones). e them with string, sprinkle with salt and epper. Brown them in 1 oz (30 g) butter, dd 1 small glass brandy, bring to the boil, and ame it. Cover, lower the heat, and cook owly for about ½ hour. Take the birds from e pan, remove string and keep warm. Put the pan 1 tablespoon chopped onion, ½ lb 225 g) sliced mushrooms, 6 oz (175 g) tomaoes, peeled and chopped, 1 bay leaf, and salt nd pepper to taste. Cook for 10–15 minutes, ut the pigeons back into the pan, and when ey are hot, serve them covered with the auce. Garnish with whole button mushrooms.

2

3

1

2

3

Chicken Cooked in Terracotta

Ingredients: *1 chicken (about 3 lb/1½ kg) · 8 juniper berries · 1 teaspoon peppercorns · leaves of 1 twig of rosemary · leaves of 1 twig sage · salt · 4 oz (115 g) sliced prosciutto, or salt pork, soaked in water for 1 hour and drained, or streaky bacon · 2 oz (60 g) butter or margarine in small pieces*

To garnish: *twigs of rosemary*

Clean (step 1), wash and dry the chicken. Crush the juniper berries and peppercorns in a mortar and chop them together with the rosemary and sage leaves. Put 1 teaspoon of the mixture inside the chicken with a pinch of salt (step 2). Arrange the prosciutto, salt pork or bacon slices around the chicken on aluminium foil. Dot with butter or margarine, and spread the remaining herb mixture over the chicken. Sprinkle liberally with salt and close the aluminium foil (step 3). Put the wrapped chicken in an earthenware dish, cover, and cook in a hot oven (400°F/gas 6) for about 2 hours. Remove the dish from the oven, taking care not to break it by putting it on a cold surface. Remove the chicken, take off the aluminium foil and transfer to a warm serving dish. Arrange paper frills on the legs and garnish with twigs of rosemary. Guinea fowl may also be prepared in this way.

Chicken with Parsley

Wash and dry a 2½-lb (1¼-kg) chicken. Put in a pan the chicken neck, leg and wing tips, and gizzard, together with 1 celery stalk, 1 carrot, peeled and chopped, 1 onion, peeled and sliced, and salt and pepper to taste. Cover with water and simmer 1–2 hours. Strain. Sauté the liver in ½ oz (15 g) butter or margarine, then chop it with a generous handful parsley, and mix with 1 teaspoon grated lemon peel, 2 oz (60 g) butter, and salt and pepper to taste. Put the mixture inside the chicken, sew the opening and tie the bird with string. Sprinkle liberally with salt and pepper, and brown it on all sides over high heat in 1 oz (30 g) butter. Add som of the hot stock, cover, lower the heat, an cook very slowly for about 1 hour or unt tender, adding more stock if the chicke becomes dry. Remove the chicken from th pan, take off the string, and keep warm. If th sauce is too thin, let it reduce on high heat. Ad 4 fl oz (100 ml) single cream, and let the sauc thicken, without boiling, on moderate hea Carve the chicken, arrange on a warm servin dish and garnish with parsley sprigs. Serve th sauce separately.

tuffed Roast Chicken

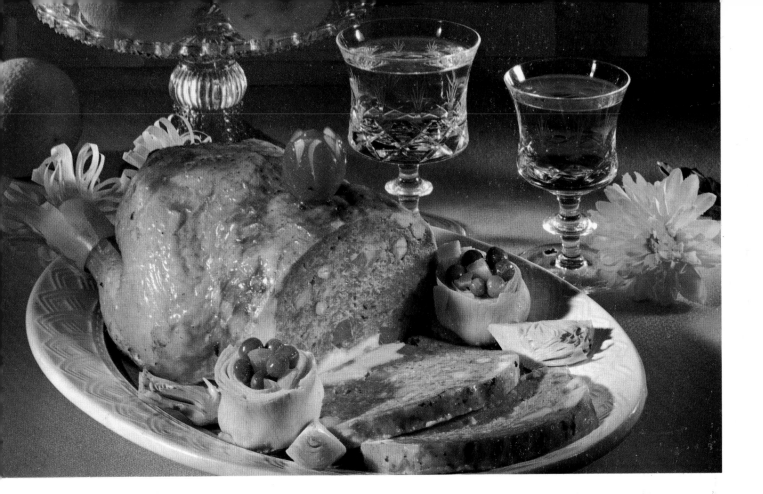

gredients: *1 chicken (about 3½ lb/1½ kg) · slice cooked ham (about 4 oz/115 g) · slice tongue (about 4 oz/115 g) · ablespoon pistachio nuts · 2 oz (60 g) tter or margarine · 1 small glass brandy*

r the stuffing: *½ lb (225 g) stewing veal · oz (115 g) pork loin · 4 oz (115 g) sausage at · 2 eggs · 2 oz (60 g) grated Parmesan eese · 1 handful white bread soaked in milk d squeezed dry · salt · pepper · mixed herbs*

garnish: *artichoke hearts · green peas · rots · radish roses (optional)*

sh and dry the chicken, cut off the tips of wings and legs. Put it on a carving board, ast side down, cut the skin with scissors m the neck to the tail (step 1), and remove bones, except for the leg bones. Spread it the board leaving the skin intact.

Prepare the stuffing: chop the veal and the pork loin, and mix in a bowl with the sausage meat, eggs, grated Parmesan cheese, white bread, and salt, pepper and mixed herbs to taste. Blend thoroughly. Cut the ham and tongue into strips. Put ½ the stuffing in the centre of the chicken (step 2), sprinkle with ½ the pistachio nuts, and arrange a layer of ½ the ham and tongue strips on top. Cover it with the remainder of the stuffing, and end with a layer of remaining pistachio nuts, ham and tongue. Fold the skin of the chicken over the stuffing, tuck the neck skin inside, and sew carefully together with string (step 3). Tie the chicken with string. Melt the butter or margarine in a roasting pan, put in the chicken, sewed side down, and brown in a moderate oven (350°F/gas 4). Bring the brandy to the boil in a pan, and flame it. Pour it quickly over the chicken, sprinkle with salt, and cook slowly for 1½–2 hours until tender, basting occasionally with the cooking juices. When cooked, remove from pan, let stand for 10 minutes, then untie and slice it. Arrange on a warm serving dish with paper frills on the legs. Garnish with artichoke hearts sautéed in butter and stuffed with green peas and carrots, and radish roses, if liked. Serve with potatoes mashed in butter and eggs and seasoned with salt, black pepper and grated nutmeg. This dish may also be served cold.

Chicken with Garlic

In a large pan with a tight-fitting lid, mix ½ glass olive oil, 4 celery stalks, chopped, and chopped parsley and salt to taste. Add 4 chicken pieces to the pan, stir, and add 40 unpeeled cloves of garlic and 1½ glasses brandy. Cover the pan and seal it with a paste made of flour and water. Put it in a moderate oven (350°F/gas 4) for about 1½ hours. Remove garlic before serving.

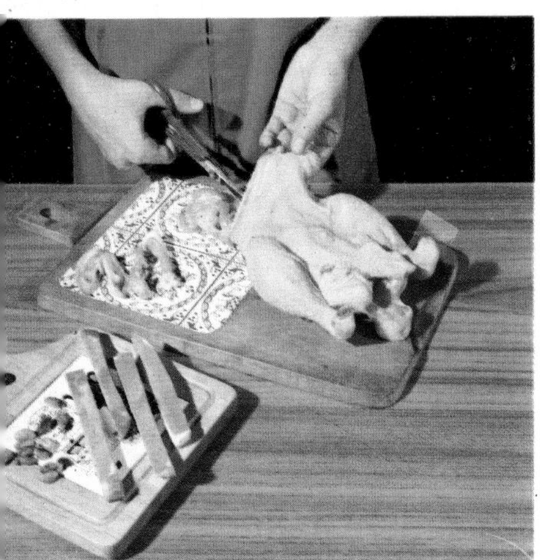

2

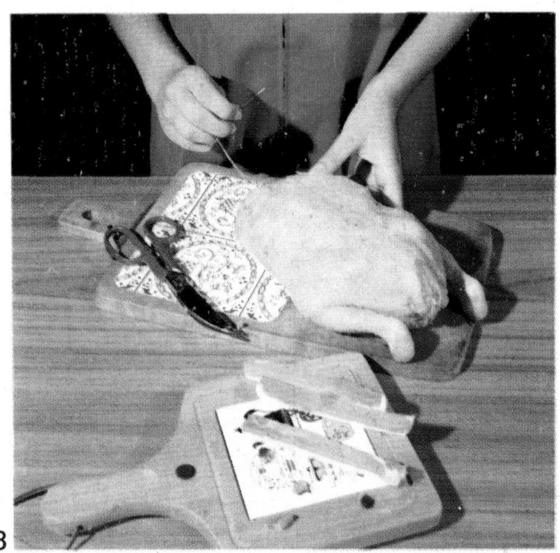

3

Turkey Stuffed with Chestnuts

Ingredients: *1 turkey (about 7 lb/3½ kg) · 2 slices salt pork soaked in water for 1 hour, or streaky bacon · 2 oz (60 g) butter · salt · pepper · ½ glass dry white wine · stock*

For the stuffing: *1¼ lb (600 g) roasted chestnuts, peeled · 2 oz (60 g) butter · ½ lb (225 g) prunes, soaked and pitted · 2 large apples · ½ lb (225 g) sausage meat*

To garnish: *chestnuts · watercress*

Wash and dry the turkey. Prepare the stuffing sauté the chestnuts in the butter (step 1) fo 10–15 minutes, together with the prunes the apples, peeled and cored, and the sausag meat, stirring occasionally. Put it inside th turkey (step 2) and sew up the opening wit string. Cover the breast with the salt pork o bacon slices (step 3) and tie the bird. Put it i a flameproof casserole with the butter in sma pieces, and brown on all sides over high hea Sprinkle liberally with salt and pepper, add th wine, let it reduce, and add some stock. Cover lower the heat, and cook for about 2 hours, c until turkey is tender, basting occasionall with the cooking juices and adding stock if th meat becomes too dry. Remove the cover fc the last 10 minutes and finish cooking on hig heat. Remove turkey from pan, transfer to warm serving platter, and let stand 10 minute before untying and carving. Garnish wit whole cooked chestnuts and watercress, an decorate turkey legs with paper frills. Th turkey can also be roasted in a moderate ove (350°F/gas 4) for 2 hours. Serves 6–8.

Braised Turkey

Cut into pieces 2½ lb (1¼ kg) turkey mea Brown it in 2 oz (60 g) butter or margarin together with 2 oz (60 g) diced salt pork soaked in cold water for 1 hour and draine Add chopped celery, carrot, onion and garli Add 1 tablespoon dried mushrooms, soaked i lukewarm water, squeezed dry and mashe with 1 tablespoon flour. Blend well, and, after few minutes, add ¾ lb (340 g) tomatoes, peele and chopped, some stock, 1 bay leaf, and sa and pepper to taste. Cover, and cook slowly f about 1 hour, adding more stock if necessar

1

2

3

2

3

Game

Duck with Orange

Ingredients: *1 young duck (about 4 lb/2 kg) · salt · pepper · butter or margarine · 1 glass dry white wine · 4–5 oranges · [illegible] cup reduced stock · ½ lemon · 2 tablespoons brandy · 1 oz (30 g) sugar · 1 tablespoon vinegar*

Wash and dry the duck, and tie with string, the legs turned backwards. Sprinkle liberally with salt and pepper, and brush with melted butter or margarine. Brown on all sides over high heat in a buttered pan (step 1), cover, lower the heat and cook for about 45 minutes or until the duck is tender. Baste occasionally with a little white wine. When cooked, take out and keep warm. Cut into thin strips the rind of 2 oranges (step 2), boil them for a few minutes, drain and refresh in cold running water. Discard excess fat from the cooking juices, mix in the stock gradually, add the juice of 2–3 oranges and the ½ lemon (step 3), the brandy, and a caramel made by dissolving the sugar in the vinegar, then boiling it vigorously with the boiled orange rind. Continue cooking the sauce on low heat for 8–10 minutes until reduced. Remove string from duck, and transfer to a warm serving dish. Pour the sauce over, arranging strips of orange rind decoratively over the breast. Garnish dish with segments from remaining orange, after removing the skin, pith and membrane. Decorate the duck's legs with paper frills.

Rolled Duck with Grand Marnier

Wash and dry a 4-lb (2-kg) duck. Cut it along the back and bone it, being careful not to split the skin. Cover the inside of the flesh with prosciutto slices and very thin slices of orange, from which the skin, pith and membranes have been removed. Roll the duck and tie with string, like a roast. Brown on all sides over high heat in 2 oz (60 g) butter or margarine, cover, lower the heat, and cook for about 1¼ hours, or until tender. When cooked, take the duck out and keep warm. Discard the excess fat from the cooking juices. Put in another pan 2 oz (60 g) sugar and 1 tablespoon white vinegar. Heat slowly until sugar dissolves, bring to the boil, and when the sugar begins to caramelize add the juice of 1–2 oranges, 4 tablespoons Grand Marnier, and the grated peel of ½ orange. Continue cooking for 3–4 minutes, then add the cooking juices from the duck, and the rind of 1 orange cut into thin strips, boiled in water for 5 minutes and drained. Remove the string from the duck, slice it, and arrange on a warm serving dish. Pour the sauce over the duck.

Pheasant on Croûtes

Ingredients: *1 pheasant, preferably a hen bird (about 2½ lb/1¼ kg) • 1 bay leaf • 2 juniper berries • 2 slices prosciutto, salt pork or bacon • 2 oz (60 g) butter or margarine • salt • pepper • 1 twig rosemary (optional) • ½ glass dry white wine • 1½ tablespoons stock • bread croûtes fried in butter*

Wash and dry the pheasant. Chop the bay leaf and juniper berries together with 2 prosciutto, salt pork or bacon slices and ½ oz (15 g) butter or margarine. Add salt and pepper to taste. Shape into a ball and place inside the bird (step 1). Sew the opening with string, cover the breast with the remaining prosciutto, salt pork or bacon slices, and tie the bird with string. Brush with melted butter, sprinkle liberally with salt and pepper, put it in pan with the rosemary, if using, and brown on all sides over high heat. Pour over the wine (step 2), return to heat, let it reduce, and add the stock. Cover, and cook slowly for about 45–50 minutes or until tender, basting occasionally with the cooking juices. The cooking can also be done in a moderate oven (350°F/gas 4). Arrange the croûtes on a warm serving dish, place the pheasant (whole or carved, according to taste) over the croûtes, and pour over the cooking juices before serving (step 3). Decorate with paper frills.

Pheasant Magyar Style

Wash and dry a 2½-lb (1¼-kg) pheasant. Chop 1 bay leaf, 1 clove, 1 clove of garlic, peeled, 1 tablespoon parsley and 1 lemon slice (peeled and without pips). Put the mixture, with salt and pepper to taste, inside the bird, and sew up with string. Cover the breast with a thin slice of fresh pork fat, tie the bird with string, and sprinkle it with Hungarian Tokay wine, or a similar sweet white wine. Sprinkle liberally with salt and pepper, and put it in a casserole with a few slices of onion and mushrooms, then add 1 glass of the wine previously used and 1 glass stock. Put the casserole in a moderate oven (350°F/gas 4) for 45–50 minutes, basting from time to time with the cooking juices. Drain the pheasant, remove string, cut the bird into serving pieces, and keep it on a warm dish. Strain the sauce, removing the excess fat, reduce it on high heat if necessary, stir in 2 tablespoons redcurrant jelly, if liked, and pour over bird.

1

2

3

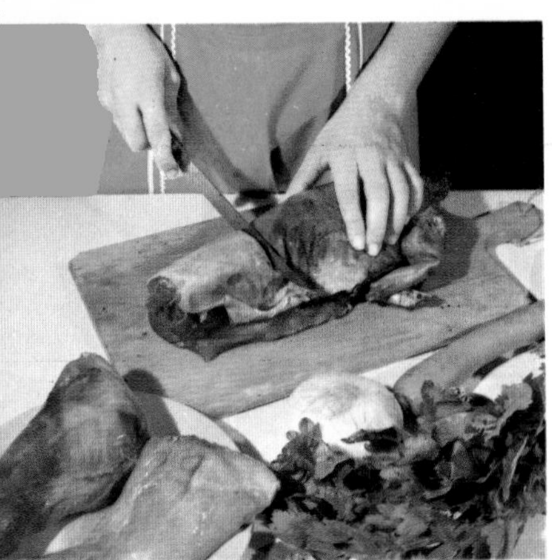

2

3

ugged Hare

gredients: *1 hare (about 7 lb/$3\frac{1}{2}$ kg) with the* *od · 2 tablespoons white wine ·* *oz (115 g) calf's liver, sliced · 2 oz (60 g)* *rk fat · 1 onion, chopped · 2 oz (60 g) butter* *margarine, or a few tablespoons oil · flour*

r the marinade: *$2\frac{1}{2}$ pints ($1\frac{1}{4}$ l) Burgundy-type* *d wine · 1 celery stalk · 1 carrot, sliced ·* *onions, chopped · 1 small bunch parsley ·* *clove of garlic, crushed · 1 bay leaf ·* *ew leaves thyme, marjoram, sage, rosemary ·* *ew juniper berries · 3–4 peppercorns ·* *cloves · 1 small stick cinnamon ·* *pinch mixed herbs and rock salt*

ash and dry the hare. Keep the blood in a owl, mixed with the white wine to prevent agulation, until blending it with the sauce the last moment. Cut the hare into serving eces (step 1), and put them in a bowl gether with the liver, heart and lung, and e calf's liver, and pour over the marinade tep 2). Let stand for 24 hours, stirring occasionally. The next day, brown in a casserole the butter, margarine or oil, pork fat and chopped onion. Drain the pieces of hare (reserving the marinade), dry them, roll lightly in flour, and put them in the casserole. Brown the meat on all sides over high heat, add all the marinade (except the livers), bring to the boil, then cover, lower the heat, and cook for about 2 hours, adding the livers after $1\frac{1}{2}$ hours. If the sauce is too thick, add some stock or hot water. A few minutes before serving take out the pieces of hare, and strain the cooking juices through a sieve (step 3). Return the sauce to the casserole, stir in the blood, add the meat, and as soon as it is hot serve with croûtes fried in butter or a polenta. Serves 10.

Braised Hare

Wash and dry 1 hare (about 7 lb/$3\frac{1}{2}$ kg). Cut into serving pieces and rub generously with salt and pepper. Put in a bowl together with $\frac{1}{2}$ cup brandy, 2 tablespoons oil, 1 chopped bay leaf, and $\frac{1}{2}$ onion, finely chopped. Marinate for 2 hours, turning the pieces over occasionally. Chop the hare's liver, place in a bowl and cover with 1 cup good red wine. Brown in a casserole 1 oz (30 g) butter, $\frac{1}{2}$ chopped onion, and 2 oz (60 g) salt pork, soaked in cold water for 1 hour, drained and chopped. Add the pieces of hare and the marinade (reserving the liver), passed through a sieve, cover, and cook very slowly for about 1 hour, adding stock if necessary. Add the chopped liver and 1 lb (500 g) sliced mushroom, and continue cooking for 1 hour, or less if the hare is tender. Transfer hare to a warm serving dish, thicken the sauce if necessary with a little beurre manié (equal quantities of butter and flour kneaded together), and pour over the hare.

Serve with bread croûtes fried in butter or a polenta. Serves 10.

1

2

3

Partridge with Grapes

Ingredients: *2 plump partridges, or 4 smaller ones · 2 (or 4) slices pork fat · butter · salt · pepper · 1 small glass brandy or $\frac{1}{2}$ glass dry white wine · $\frac{1}{4}$ lb (115 g) white grapes · stock · 4 bread croûtes fried in butter*

Wash and dry the partridges. Cover the breasts with 1 slice pork fat, and tie them with string, keeping the legs parallel with the bodies (step 1). Brush generously with melted butter, sprinkle with salt and pepper, and cook in a roasting pan in a hot oven (400°F/ gas 6) for about $\frac{1}{2}$ hour, basting from time to time with the cooking juices. Drain them and keep warm. Pour out the fat from the pan, leaving the sediments, and add the brandy or white wine. Dissolve the sediments on low heat, stirring with a wooden spoon. Peel the grapes, remove the pips, and put the grapes in the pan with the partridges (step 2). After a few minutes, add a few tablespoons stock and 1 oz (30 g) butter. Reduce the juice over high heat, strain it to separate the grapes, and keep it warm. Garnish the serving dish with the fried croûtes, put in the partridges, after removing string and the grapes (step 3) and serve with the cooking juices in a separate dish.

Partridge Polish Style

Wash and dry 2 partridges. Sauté for a few minutes in a skillet the partridges' livers with 1 oz (30 g) butter or margarine, 1 chopped spring onion, 1 tablespoon chopped parsley, $\frac{1}{2}$ bay leaf, salt and pepper to taste. Remove the bay leaf, and pass the other ingredients through a sieve. Put a little of the mixture inside each bird, and sew up with string. Cover the breasts with slices of salt pork, soaked in cold water for 1 hour and drained, or bacon, according to taste, and tie the birds with string. Put the in a casserole with $1\frac{1}{2}$ tablespoons stock. P the casserole in a moderate oven (350°F/g 4), and cook for $\frac{1}{2}$ hour, basting from time time with the cooking juices. You may also co them on top of the stove, browning them fir in butter, and adding stock gradually required. Take partridges from casserol remove string and cut the partridges in ha Arrange them on a warm serving dis pour over the cooking juices and sprinkle wi 1 tablespoon breadcrumbs lightly browned i butter. Garnish with lemon quarters ar parsley.

2

3

quabs with Truffles

gredients: *4 squabs (young pigeons) • salt • pper • truffles • 4 slices prosciutto, or lean lt pork soaked in cold water for 1 hour and ained • 3 oz (90 g) butter or margarine • glass brandy • a few tablespoons stock or ter*

garnish: *parsley sprigs*

'ash and dry the squabs, sprinkle with salt d pepper, and put inside each thin slices of uffle (step 1). Wrap them in prosciutto or lt pork slices, tie them with string (step 2), d brown in butter or margarine. Pour over e brandy, bring to the boil, flame, and add the ater or stock, and cook for 25–35 minutes until tender. Remove from the pan, untie, range them on piped mashed potatoes or sotto, and keep warm. Add chopped truffle the cooking juices (step 3), heat slowly for a few minutes, stirring well. Pour over the squabs, garnish with parsley sprigs and serve immediately.

Squabs en Brochette

Wash and dry 4 young squabs. Put them on oiled wooden or metal skewers, alternating each one with a piece of pork fat (blanched for 5 minutes in boiling water) and a piece of mushroom. Place the skewers in a buttered roasting pan, season with salt and pepper to taste, and pour over melted butter. Cook in a very hot oven (450°F/gas 8) for 10 minutes. Take out the pan, sprinkle the birds with crumbs of white bread and baste them with the cooking juices. Put the pan back into the oven, and continue cooking for another 5–6 minutes. Remove the skewers, and arrange the birds on a warm serving dish. Pour into the pan 1 small glass brandy, bring to the boil, flame, and reduce the juices. Pour over the birds and serve immediately.

Squabs with Juniper Berries

Wash and dry 4 young squabs. Put inside each bird salt and pepper to taste, 1 small piece butter, and 3 crushed juniper berries. Wrap each bird in 1 slice pork fat, tie with string, and put in a buttered skillet. Brown on all sides over high heat, lower the heat, and cook for 15–20 minutes. Arrange on bread croûtes on a warm serving dish. Dissolve the cooking sediments with a little stock and pour over the birds.

1

2

3

Assorted Meat Dishes

Italian Pot-au-feu

Ingredients: *3 quarts (3 l) water · 1 tablespoon rock salt · 2 lb (1 kg) stewing beef in the slice · 1 carrot, peeled and sliced · 1 onion, peeled and sliced · 1 celery stalk · 1 clove of garlic, crushed · 1 small tomato, quartered (optional) · 1¼ lb (600 g) stewing veal in the slice · 1 calf's foot · a few potatoes (optional)*

Bring the water and rock salt to the boil, add the beef (step 1), and skim the scum (step 2). For a richer stock, put the meat in cold rather than boiling water. Add the vegetables and continue cooking for 3 hours. Add the veal and the calf's foot halfway through the cooking (step 3). Add the potatoes, if liked, ½ hour before the cooking is completed. Remove meats from pan, slice, and arrange on a warm serving dish. Pour over 1½ tablespoons of the boiling stock. Serve with the vegetables and various sauces to taste, such as ketchup, mustard, green sauce and pickles. You may also add other meats, such as ½ chicken or capon, or garlic sausage cooked separately for 1 hour. Serves 7–8.

Boiled Meat with Tuna Sauce

Cut ¾ lb (340 g) boiled meat (veal or beef) into thin slices, and arrange them on a shallow dish. Prepare a mayonnaise with 1 egg yo 6 fl oz (150 ml) oil, the juice of 1 lemon, and s and pepper. Mix it with 6 oz (175 g) tuna fish oil, 2 anchovy fillets, desalted, and a few cape all worked through a sieve. Dilute the sau with a few tablespoons cold stock. Pour over the meat, and garnish with slices lemon and red peppers.

Boiled Beef au Gratin

Cut into thin slices, or chop roughly, ¾ lb (340 boiled beef. Put it in a buttered ovenproof dis Cover with tomato sauce, seasoned wi chopped onions and mixed with chopp parsley and basil. Add a layer of mash potato, and sprinkle with breadcrumbs ar grated Gruyère cheese in equal proportion Dot with butter. Put the dish in a hot ov (400°F/gas 6) for 15–20 minutes, or until golden crust has formed. Serve immediately i the same dish.

ᐟowl and Spinach ᐟudding

ngredients: *½ lb (225 g) breast of chicken and lb (225 g) breast of turkey, uncooked, or lb (500 g) cooked chicken and turkey meat · ' lb (1 kg) fresh, or ¼ lb (115 g) frozen pinach · butter or margarine · 1 sliced onion · tablespoon brandy · salt · pepper · grated ·utmeg · mixed herbs · 4 oz (115 g) white read without crust, soaked in milk, squeezed 'ry and worked through a sieve · 3 egg yolks · egg white · 8 fl oz (225 ml) single cream · - oz (115 g) grated Parmesan cheese · readcrumbs*

'o garnish: *creamed carrots · parsley*

using fresh spinach, wash and cook in salted oiling water until tender (5–10 minutes). ' using frozen spinach, cook according to ackage instructions. Pass spinach through a egetable mill and sauté lightly in melted utter or margarine. Cut the chicken and ırkey into small pieces (step 1). Melt 1 table- ›oon butter or margarine, add the onion and ıuté until golden; discard the onion. Add the ıeat and sauté lightly. Add the brandy, bring › the boil, flame it, then add salt and pepper to ıste, 1 pinch nutmeg and mixed herbs and ›ntinue cooking slowly for 10–15 minutes. ass the meat through a meat-grinder, and ıix it with the bread, eggs, spinach, cream and ·rated Parmesan cheese, adding more salt and ıixed herbs to taste (step 2). Butter generously ı ovenproof dish, 8 inches in diameter and inches high, a pastry mould, or a pastry ring, ıd sprinkle with breadcrumbs. Pour in the ·epared mixture. Insert and remove the lade of a knife to allow air to penetrate during ›oking (step 3). Put in a moderate oven ;50°F/gas 4) and cook for about 1 hour or ıtil the blade of a knife inserted in the ıdding comes out clean. Remove from the ·at and unmould. Arrange in the centre of ıe pudding and around it creamed carrots, ·ssed in chopped parsley.

'eal and Cream Pudding

·rown lightly in 1 oz (30 g) butter or marga- ıne 1 lb (500 g) stewing veal in the slice. ·ason with salt. Add some stock, cover and ›ok for 1 hour. Mince, mix with 3 eggs, fl oz (225 ml) single cream, 4 oz (115 g) ated Parmesan cheese, and cook as above.

2

3

1

2

3

Fritto Misto

Ingredients: *4 oz (115 g) chicken · 4 oz (115 g) veal · 4 oz (115 g) pork · 2 oz (60 g) butter · salt · grated nutmeg · 2 tablespoons Marsala · 4 oz (115 g) sweetbreads · 4 oz (115 g) chicken livers · 1 thick slice each of prosciutto and mortadella · 4 oz (115 g) Gruyére cheese · hot béchamel sauce prepared with 3 oz (90 g) butter, 6 oz (175 g) flour, 3 cups milk, salt and grated nutmeg to taste, with 1 egg yolk added · 2 eggs · breadcrumbs · oil*

To garnish: *parsley sprigs · lemon wedges*

Cut the chicken, veal and pork into cubes. Brown in butter, add salt and grated nutmeg and the Marsala and continue cooking. Meanwhile, blanch the sweetbreads and chicken livers. When they are cold cut them into cubes of the same size as the meats and add to the pan. Cut the prosciutto, mortadella and Gruyère cheese into cubes, add them to the pan and stir well. When meats are tender remove all ingredients from pan and string on small oiled wooden or metal skewers, alternating the different ingredients. Dip the skewers in the hot béchamel sauce, put them on a buttered dish, and let them cool. Roll them carefully and serve on a warm dish (step 1), and fry them in deep hot oil. Drain them carefully and serve on a warm dish together with a selection of the meats and vegetables described below. Garnish with parsley sprigs and lemon wedges.

Fried Artichokes

Discard the hard outer leaves of 4 artichokes, quarter them, and let stand for a few minutes in water and lemon juice. Drain them, dry, cover in beaten egg, then in breadcrumbs (step 2) and fry them in hot oil until golden.

Fried Brains and Beef Marrow

Prepare the brains and marrow for cooking, cut them into pieces, roll them in flour, then in beaten egg and breadcrumbs, and fry in butter. You may also dip them in batter, made of water, flour, cheese and egg, and fry them.

Chicken Croquettes

Chop 1 lb (500 g) cooked chicken togeth with 2 oz (60 g) prosciutto or salami. Prepa a béchamel sauce with $1\frac{1}{2}$ oz (45 g) butte 2 oz (60 g) flour, 6 fl oz (150 ml) milk, sa and nutmeg. Remove the sauce from th heat, add the chicken and prosciutto salami, 2 tablespoons grated Parmesan chees chopped parsley and 1 egg yolk. Pour th mixture on a buttered board and spread it obtain a 1-inch layer. Let it cool, cut in pieces, and make into croquette shap $2\frac{1}{2}$ inches long and $\frac{1}{2}$ inch in diamete Roll them in flour, then in beaten egg ar breadcrumbs (step 3), and brown and coc them in deep hot oil. Take them out with slotted spoon, and drain them on paper towel

Fried Zucchini

Cut zucchini lengthwise in thin slices, dr them, roll them in flour, then in egg an breadcrumbs, and fry in deep hot oil. Othe vegetables can also be prepared in this manne

lixed Grill

gredients: *4 lamb cutlets · 2 veal kidneys · slices calf's liver · 2 sausages · $\frac{1}{2}$ chicken · tter or oil · $\frac{1}{4}$ pint (125 ml) boiling stock · tablespoons oil · 1 tablespoon tomato chup · $\frac{1}{2}$ teaspoon Worcestershire sauce · love of garlic and 1 spring onion, chopped · t · pepper*

make the lamb cutlets tastier let them stand 2–3 hours in a marinade prepared with tablespoons oil, 3 tablespoons vinegar, crushed clove of garlic, 4 chopped mint ves and salt and pepper to taste. Halve the neys, remove the core, slice the liver (step 1), d brush with butter or oil and put on a hot ll. Cook for 2–3 minutes on each side. Cook sausages but do not brush them with fat. Meanwhile, bring to the boil the stock mixed h 2 tablespoons oil, the tomato ketchup, rcestershire sauce, garlic and spring onion xture, and salt and pepper, and continue king for 6–8 minutes. Brush the chicken h the sauce and put it on the hot grill h the skin uppermost (step 2). Cook for –35 minutes, turning and brushing with sauce occasionally. Drain the cutlets, erving the marinade, and put them on the ll. Cook for 12–15 minutes, turning them l brushing with the marinade.

illed Piquant Steak

x in a bowl 6 oz (175 g) Gorgonzola or quefort cheese together with 3–4 tableons oil, 1 mashed clove of garlic and 1 lespoon brandy or whisky. Grill over charl, or under the grill 2 ribs of beef, each –1$\frac{1}{2}$ lb (about 600 g). Spread the cheese xture over them and serve when it melts.

babs Eastern Style

pare a marinade with 1 cup pineapple ce, $\frac{1}{2}$ mashed clove of garlic, and 1$\frac{1}{2}$ lespoons soy or Worcestershire sauce. Cut lb (600 g) lamb into 2-inch cubes, and let nd in the marinade for 2$\frac{1}{2}$ hours. String m on small, oiled metal skewers, alternating h pineapple pieces (step 3) and grill.

eak with Mustard Sauce

sh with oil 4 ribs of beef or veal slices, and k on a hot grill, over a dripping pan, or in an iron pan. When they are cooked to taste, remove them and keep them warm. If the cooking has been done on a grill gather the cooking juices, discarding excess fat, and put them in a pan. Add 1 tablespoon strong mustard, $\frac{1}{2}$ glass dry white wine, let it reduce on high heat, then add 8 fl oz (225 ml) single cream, lowering the heat until sauce has thickened. Do not let boil. Add 1 small glass brandy, and put back the meat to re-heat it. Serve on a warm dish together with the mustard sauce served separately.

2

3

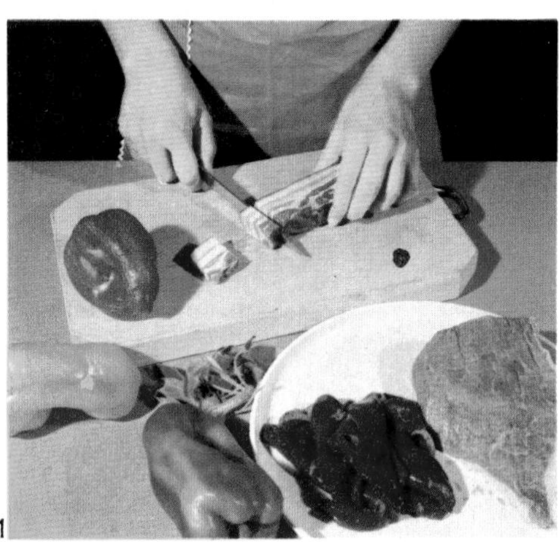

1

2

3

Brochettes Maison

Ingredients: *10 oz (300 g) veal · 10 oz (300 g) calf's liver · 4 oz (115 g) salt pork in the slice, soaked in cold water for 1 hour and drained · 1 red pepper and 1 green or yellow pepper (fresh or canned) · sage leaves · 2 oz (60 g) butter or margarine · salt · pepper · ½ glass dry white wine · stock*

To garnish: *lemon slices · lettuce (optional)*

Cut the meat, liver, salt pork and peppers in equal pieces. String them with the sage leaves on oiled wooden or metal skewers, alternating the ingredients (step 2). Brown on all sides over high heat in the butter or margarine (step 3). Season with salt and pepper to taste, add the white wine, let it reduce, add the stock, lower the heat and cook slowly or until meats are tender. Serve with the reduced cooking juices. The cooking can also be done under the grill. Garnish with lemon and lettuce.

Veal en Brochette

Cut 1½ lb (750 g) veal into 1-inch cubes. Marinate them for 1½ hours in a mixture of oil, lemon juice and salt. String on oiled wooden or metal skewers, alternating with sage leaves and diced salt pork, soaked in cold water for 1 hour and drained. Cook on charcoal or under the grill until tender, turning and basting with the marinade.

Shish Kebab

Cut 1¼ lb (600 g) lamb (leg is the most suitable cut for this) into 2-inch cubes. Let them stand for 1½ hours in a marinade prepared in the following manner: mix together 2 tablespoons oil, the juice of 1 lemon, 1 tablespoon chilli powder (or 1 pinch paprika), 1 tablespoon finely chopped onion, 1 mashed clove of garlic, 1 pinch ginger, 1 pinch salt and 1 teaspoon curry powder. Drain lamb and disc marinade. String the pieces of lamb on lc oiled wooden or metal skewers, alternat with pieces of onion, peppers, mushroom c and halves of tomatoes. Cook over charc or under the grill until lamb is tender.

Chinese Brochettes

Cut 1½ lb (750 g) pork (loin, fillet or leg the most suitable cuts) into 1½-inch cubes. stand for 3 hours in a marinade prepared follows: mix together 2 tablespoons soy Worcestershire sauce, 2 tablespoons dry M sala, ½ teaspoon sugar and ½ clove of gar peeled. Drain pork, reserving the marina String the pieces of pork on oiled me skewers and cook very slowly over charc or under the grill until tender and cook through, turning and brushing from ti to time with the marinade.